Dr. (Lt.) Sandhya Rani Mohanty

Introduction to Home Management

Anchor Academic
Publishing

Mohanty, Sandhya Rani, Dr. (Lt.): Introduction to Home Management, Hamburg, Anchor Academic Publishing 2016

Buch-ISBN: 978-3-96067-029-2
PDF-eBook-ISBN: 978-3-96067-529-7
Druck/Herstellung: Anchor Academic Publishing, Hamburg, 2016

Bibliografische Information der Deutschen Nationalbibliothek:
Die Deutsche Nationalbibliothek verzeichnet diese Publikation in der Deutschen
Nationalbibliografie; detaillierte bibliografische Daten sind im Internet über
http://dnb.d-nb.de abrufbar.

Bibliographical Information of the German National Library:
The German National Library lists this publication in the German National Bibliography.
Detailed bibliographic data can be found at: http://dnb.d-nb.de

© Anchor Academic Publishing, Imprint der Diplomica Verlag GmbH
Hermannstal 119k, 22119 Hamburg
http://www.diplomica-verlag.de, Hamburg 2016
Printed in Germany

Dedicated to my father

Table of Contents

Chapter 1
Home Management

1.1 Meaning

The term 'Home Management' was coined by Maria Parloa in 1880. When she first used the term, it simply meant anything that needed to be accomplished within the household.

As this discipline began to develop, the specific fields of study began to emerge. The principles and concepts of home management began to emerge. The definition of what home management is and how it is used in daily life took on new directions and meaning. Every individual has values, goals and standards. Effective management means recognizing values, understanding decision making and factors affecting decision making, determining long term and short term goals as well as allocating resources to attain these goals.

1.1.1 Concept of Management

Management plays important role in day-to-day life. Each individual needs to have knowledge of managing activities. It is integral part of human life. Family life is full of various goals and achievements whether it is an individual goal or achievement or a family goal. Most of time, it is essential for family members to take wise decisions regarding education, career, marriage of members in the family depending on their values and goals. There are specifically two concepts of management.

The first is the materialistic concept and the second is the Human concept.

Human Concept: Here emphasis has been given to all round development of the family members. Maximum use of available resources is made on each member of the family. Importance is given to human needs. Instead of taking paid help, the homemaker cooks food for the family, with special care. In case of emergency the homemaker use to simplify work by using shortcut methods of cooking or changing the menu. While doing this, many times, standards have been adjusted to suit the changing situation. Effective use of available resources, human as well as non-human, affects the quality of life.

Materialistic Concept: According to the materialistic concept of home management the efficiency in doing work and standardization of work is important. By doing this quality of work is improved and more perfection is maintained. Homemakers or managers try to maintain the standard for maintaining standard they spend more money. For example, if the woman working outside, she will prefer paid help for getting the work done as per the family standards. If the family is having very high standard of cleanliness, i.e.

cleaning of the house twice a day, she will take paid help to complete the work. The importance given to the standard of work is mainly highlighted. In other words, it is a process consisting of planning, organizing, implementing (controlling), evaluating and accomplishing stated objectives by the use of resources.

Home management is the vital factor in every family contributing to the overall health, happiness and well being of the family. Management today is an important factor in every sphere of activity. The concept of management deals with achieving desired goals through planned activity. It is an essential component of family living. Home management is the natural outcome of human relationship in the home environment. When the family is established, management becomes one of the major responsibilities of the family living.

Home management deals with the practical application of the principles of management to the home. Home management is the administrative aspect of family living. The study of Home management is intimately linked with values, standards and goals which give meaning to the lives, thoughts, feelings and experiences of the members of the family. These values, standards and goals which are closely related to each other, motivate the family to make decisions, to achieve their desired goals.

1.1.2 Definition of Home Management

According to Godjousson, "Household management is in all countries, the most common occupation employing the most people, handling the most money and is of fundamental importance for the health of the people."

Gross and Crandall describe Home management in its simplest terms as "using what you have to get what you want."

According to Kotzin, "Home management is a practical science. In home management, managing shows some degree of competence. A home in which goals are being attained with some degree of satisfaction may be considered a well managed home."

According to Nickel and Dorsey, "Home management is planning, controlling and evaluating the use of resources of the family for the purpose of attaining family goals."

This can be represented as follows:

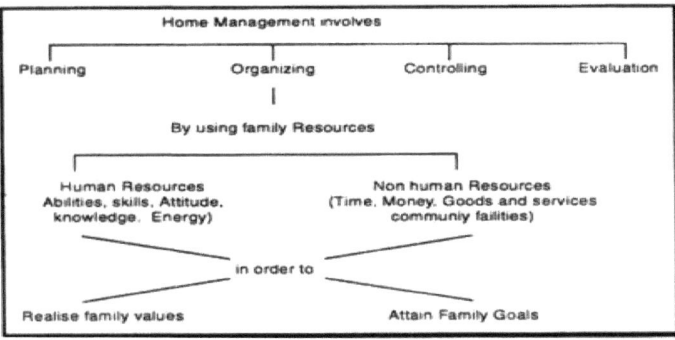

Fig: 1

Effective management enhances the chances of reaching the desired goals through wise decisions and effective use of resources.

According to R.P. Devdas, "Home management is making the best use of what you have to get what you want." What you have" means the resources available in the family and "What you want to get" meaning to goals or aims of the family. All the resources (Both human and non-human) which are available for a particular family must be utilized properly in order to achieve the family goals.

Devdas compared home management to a Dam and the resources with Rain water. Rain water is deposited in a Dam and is utilized for water supply, electricity and irrigation purposes at the time of necessity. Just like that all human and non-human resources are deposited in the DAM of Home Management. They are utilized for building a house, education and marriage of children and for various other purposes. By utilizing the resources the family goals can be achieved. The definition of Devdas is represented with a diagram.

Devdas's Definition of Home Management:

In simple terms, Home management is a family working together for common purposes, the forming of plan of action, the sharing of responsibilities the organized and controlled use of available resources. It involves homemaker's managerial ability, her interest, capacity to motivate the other members of the family, to work to achieve a common goal for the development of the family. Effective management enhances the chances of achieving goals by making wise decisions and proper utilization of resources.

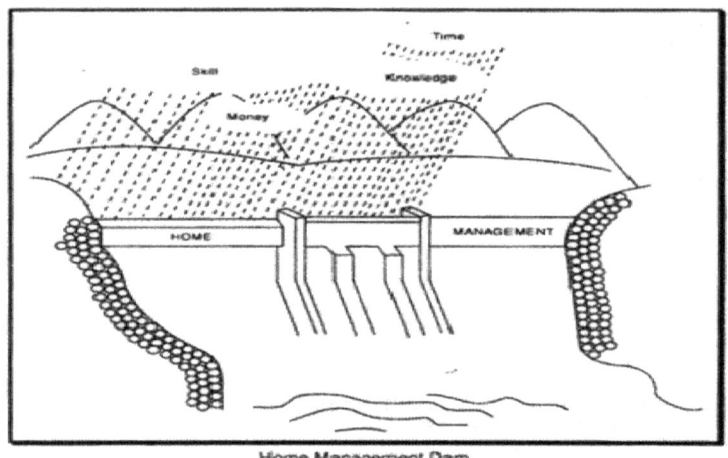

Home Management Dam

Fig:2

A well managed home is one in which the homemaker having acquired a degree of competence, works towards well defined goals or objectives. These when achieved provide her with a sense of satisfaction. A homemaker functions as a producer, consumer and co-ordinate of various activities to be carried out to achieve family goals. She manages the house in such a way that all the members of the family are satisfied and family can achieve the goals.

The changes in our life have an influence on the management of the home in today's life. The process of management becomes a rational and intelligent method of dealing with change. It is not only the intelligent use of resources and the satisfaction that is obtained that matters in the modern family, but the all round development of family members and their welfare as well. Therefore a systematic knowledge of Home management is needed by homemakers. The efficient management requires specialized knowledge, wide experiences and new type of skills.

1.1.3 Need for Home Management

Management plays a significant role in shaping our lives. With the changing environment, the need for management also becomes inevitable to identify and deal with problems, which emerge from change. Effective management in the home depends to a large extent on the managerial ability, interest and leadership quality of the homemaker and also their ability to motive the family members in the right direction for achieving desired goals. To the homemaker, who wants to manage her home properly and efficiently, knowledge of home management is helpful and essential.

In our modern technological environment, where situations are complex and highly flexible, where many choices are possible and where values of changes more rapidly, the need for management is essential. The homemaker in order to carry out every day's works without much strain and tension should know about the various aspects of home making.

It comprises the study of:

1. Planning and organization of action and the control and utilization of the various resources of the home for the proper benefit of the members of the family.

2. Family economy and the method of proper distribution of family income.

3. All aspects of home making such as meal planning the proper choice of foods in relationship to cost and requirements, the selection and construction of clothing, laundering, child care and the care and maintenance of household equipment's.

Home management makes use of findings of science and knowledge of the different aspects of family life, economic, social, psychological, physicals, spiritual and technological. It applies this knowledge to the use of family resources to meet living situations, to solve problems and help resolve conflict.

1.2   Roles and Responsibilities of a **Home Maker**

Similar to any business organization the management roles are required for the home maker to be efficient, effective and successful. To be an effective manager, the homemaker must possess special qualities for being effective and efficient. This is especially important because she wants to run the home smoothly. An efficient homemaker will have the ability to get things done correctly. She needs to know the optimum utilisation of resources both human as well as non-human resources.

1.3   Interpersonal Roles of a Home Maker

The various interpersonal roles of a homemaker as the manager in the home include the following:

- Guiding the family towards development of a sound philosophy of life.
- Channelizing personal relationships 'which are wholesome and satisfying.
- Taking care of children and their needs such as feeding, bathing, cleaning, clothing etc.

- Inculcate ethical habits and qualities among the family members such as tolerance, patience, cooperation, harmony, love and sympathy, and develop satisfying relationship within and outside the family.
- Appreciation of differences as means of enriching life, and. an all round personality development.
- Planning for participation of family members in community activities as responsible citizens
- Acceptance of mutual responsibility for family and community.
- Informational Roles of Home Manager
- The informational roles of the manager in the home are
- Developing a sound philosophy with sustaining values.
- Planning for and providing nutritious food and suitable housing and clothing for the family.
- Planning for and helping to maintain health of the family members by keeping the knowledge of the human body, mental health, family planning, formation of good habits and care of the sick and the old people and of first aid which can be utilised during emergencies.
- Planning for and guiding the educational and social development of the members of the family.
- Making the family members aware of the various 'public facilities' or community resources such as the water supply, electricity, cooking gas, telephones, hospitals, transport, public parks, library etc., and their judicious use.
- Giving knowledge about the various local services available in case of emergencies, such as fire, theft, accident, death etc.
- Disseminating the information about the various social orginisations like Resident Welfare Associations, Mahila Mandals, Mahila Samitis,Yuvak Kendras, Panchyats and community centers.

1.4   Decisional roles

The manager in the home is expected to perform the following decisional roles also:

- Setting family goals.
- Planning the family members' time and energy resources in such a ways that the work is done and their demands are satisfied.

- Planning and guiding the use of family income, bringing a balance between income and expenditure, supplementing family income, besides saving money for the future etc.
- Planning for and providing for the family, which will meet the day-to-day needs of its members.
- Planning for purchasing equipment and furnishings for the home.

Being aware of her rights and responsibilities as a consumer, this shall enable her to use her knowledge to choose the best of her ability to select the right quality product in the right quantity at the right time for the right price.

The managerial responsibilities as mentioned so far are all interrelated. For example, family finances and their management touch all phases of life as they influence the desires, decisions and choices of all the family members.

To be able to accomplish the daily household work without undue strain and tension, the housewife should think of each managerial responsibility and task to relate to it in terms of time and effort required for their accomplishment.

1.5   Qualities of a Home Maker

The home maker to be a successful manager should have certain qualities as given by Premavathy et.al, 2005. They are

Intelligence: An intelligent manager is keen on observing, understanding, thinking and remembering. She should develop all ways of gaining knowledge, ability to solve problems and achieve goals. Intelligence also includes mental alertness and ability to grasp knowledge and situation.

Enthusiasm: It is an ability to motivate others to become interested in the activity. The environment created should be contagious and make everyone to take interest in performing and completing the work. An enthusiastic manager can create a feeling of happiness by working hard to achieve her targets.

Imagination: This is the ability to rearrange facts and ideas into new patterns of work. This aids in making fresh plans and come out successfully in meeting problem situations. It can also be called creativity.

Perseverance: A good manager should have the ability to combine courage and patience to face facts. She has to believe in the inherent values of the task and feel strong about the outcome of the efforts. Faith in work and abilities will give the manager the courage to take necessary risks and try to achieve solutions until the problems are solved and goals are achieved.

Judgment: A sense of judgment enables the manager to be fair in weighing the various facts in a situation and to see the problem in totality. She should be able to weigh critically and make decisions while choosing the best alternative.

Adaptability: The human environment and the work demands are not static and require change in the approaches. All managers have to adapt themselves and their approaches as and when required. An intelligent manager will be able to adapt quickly in changing situations and changing demands.

Communication: A manger should be able to convey clearly and have a meaningful dialogue with the family members. This not only involves sharing of knowledge, feelings, desires and experiences, but also taking time to share thoughts with one another. An effective communication is the key to managers' success.

Understanding Human Nature for Team Building and Leadership: The managers should be sympathetic and understanding since these are important in developing healthy human relationships and for reducing friction while dealing with others. The manager has to understand the values, attitudes, behaviour and capabilities of the family members so that she is able to delegate the right responsibility to the right person and lead and motivate them towards the achievement of goals.

Self-Confidence and Self-Esteem: They are important qualities of a manager which helps in decision-making and leading the whole family towards their goals. A confident person with the faith in herself and her team can easily lead the family towards success.

Synergy: A manager can use synergy by combining and coordinating the individual capacities to achieve higher total output. When human efforts are combined, the total efforts are much more than the addition of their individual efforts. This is synergy.

1.6   Characteristics of a Home Maker

The eminent management expert, Fayol lists the following characteristics of a manager. These characteristics help her in doing her job effectively. These characteristics are more apparent and help a person to easily recognise and distinguish herself as a good manager. They form important guidelines for efficient and effective managers.

Physical Health: A manager has to a have a good physical health and vigour to perform the duties properly. In the absence of a good physical health, the manager is not i a position to carry out the work successfully. A healthy mind lives in a healthy body.

Mental Health: Similar to good physical health, it is important to have good mental health too. It provides the manager the ability to learn, understand and judge in logical and unbiased manner. A good mental health also aids in adopting oneself in changing situations.

Moral Responsibility: This includes the characteristics such as being firm, willing, loyal, dignified and factual. The other moral values like teamwork, sincerity, honesty and justice are of equal importance as they help managers in securing the faith of their boss, subordinates or family members.

Educational Qualification: A manager needs to be knowledgeable and informative. An educated person can allocate resources better and can be a better negotiator than a one with lesser education.

Technical Knowledge: A good technical knowledge is an important aspect of management. A manager needs to know all about the functional and operational areas of her organisation. It is essential for a manager to be equipped with the latest technical knowledge as it gives her an extra edge in her' field. Also a manager with thorough technical knowledge can monitor and supervise better. She can also work out newer and better technical solution to problems by developing new alternatives. As management has become a specialised field, managers of each field must have knowledge of her field i.e. a finance manager must know about all technical aspect of finances and similarly, a sales and advertising manager should have knowledge of media, communication skills and a home manager should have full knowledge of managing family finances, child care, meal management, clothing etc.

Work Experience: Experience is richer than qualifications. While an educational qualification provides a theoretical knowledge, experience provides her the practical solutions, thus enabling her to face and tackle challenges and come out of it successfully. Experience to some extent can make up for the lack of education. It acts as self-educator.

Thus it can be seen that a manager need to be a master as well as a jack of all trades. The success of a manager depends entirely upon how well and quickly she develops these qualities. These qualities and characteristics are of great help to a manager in performing her function. Now let us have a look at various functions of a manager in any organisation may it be business or home.

References
1. Varghese, M. A., Ogale n. N. and Srinivasan K. 1985, Home Management, New Age International (P) Limited, Publishers New Delhi.
2. Premavathy Seetharaman, Sonia Batra and Preeti Mehra 2005,
3. An Introduction to Family Resource Management, CBS Publishers and Distributors, New Delhi
4. http://jborolandlady.wordpress.com/2010/07/05/homemaker-qualities/
5. http://www.yourarticlelibrary.com/home-management/homemanagement-meaning-concept-and-needs/47779/
6. http://www.familyresourcemanagement.org/services/management/#sthash.MIkwrTkZ.dpuf
7. http://ecoursesonline.iasri.res.in/course/view.php?id=218
8. http://www.familyresourcemanagement.org/services/management/#sthash.MIkwrTkZ.dpuf

Chapter 2
Family Resources

Family resources, meaning & importance of resources,
Classifications (human and non human), characteristics of resources,
Factors affecting resource use

Introduction

In management resources play a very crucial and important role. Resources are used by the family to make decision for achieving the goals of the family. Without resources, the process of decision making is ineffective. Resources should be used in such a way, so that maximum satisfaction is attained by the family. Decisions an optimum allocation of resources is a must in management for attaining the desired goals.

Every individual and family has a number of resources available which may or may not be used by the family to the fullest extent. Sometimes the individual or the family may not be aware of these resources. They vary for individuals, communities, states and nations. However all types of resources are used to achieve the family goals.

2.1   Meaning and Definition of Resources

Resources can be defined as the means which are available and recognized for their potential in meeting demands. Means are those things which are instrumental in reaching the desired ends (Maloch and Decan).

Similarly Betty B. Swanson defined resources as tangible and intangible components which one uses to achieve goals, objectives and to meet demands.

According to Random House Dictionary of the English language, 'resource' is a source of supply, support or aid, especially one holds in reserve" and "has the capability in dealing with a situation or in meeting difficulties"

Nickel et al (1976) defined resources as "the assets that can be used to accomplish goals". The three important words are 'assets', 'used' and 'goals' that play an important role in the identification of resources. Assets are the monetary items such as money, savings, income or personal property having exchange value. All resources have the use and resources are used to achieve the set goals by the family.

Gross, Crandall and knoll stressed the availability of resources by defining them as they are those available means which are used for reaching goals and meeting demands.

Deacon and Firebaugh defined the resources as 'they are the supply reservoir for use in the system's specific action and are necessary in some form to solve every management problem.

2.2   Classification of Resources

(A.) The resources are classified in a number of ways. The first type of classification is in to two main groups based on their point of origin. They are:

1. Human Resources:

Human resources are less tangible and can be easily determined. These resources are used for productive purpose. They Originate internally and constitute the personal characteristics and attributes. Human resources cannot be utilized independently of the individual. These are the resources available to you as a person you have become, in terms of education, occupational status, skills, attitude, traits, and other personal characteristics.

Knowledge has no ends and is acquired at every step. In the home it can be selecting right and proper food at proper time of the year. The home maker should be alert in knowing the new ways of managing her household.

Abilities are inherent and they can also be acquired during life time through education and concious efforts. Skills are the ways of doings things or works perfectly. Skills and abilities range from cooking, knitting, interior decoration to creating art.

Attitudes and interests help in achieving the goals comfortably and make the person unique irrespective of caste, creed and status. All other human resource decides how effectively one utilizes the time resource.

Energy is needed to each and every task or activity. It is needed to carry out the vital physiological and metabolic activities such as breathing, blood circulation, digestion etc. It is very important to use energy effectively for the attainment of goals.

The human resources of any individual are clearly both interrelated and interdependent.

Example: The increased knowledge may increase one's confidence to move ahead quickly or make one aware of the risks and be cautious than before.

2. Non Human resources:

Non human resources are external to the individual but are possessed, utilized or controlled by the family. These resources are very much essential for the achievement of goals and are limited in their availability.

Non-human resources include the personal possessions, family possessions and the resources available to the individual with his/her community, state and nation. Money is the purchasing power, used to get other resources or achieve goals or attain satisfaction.

It is an important and major nonhuman resource which has the power to purchase other resources and achieve the desired goals. The material goods that each individual or the family possesses are varied and different. They range from safety pins to the house, in which the family lives, from clothing to pens, from perishable foods to current novels, from fuel oil to furniture etc.

The community facilities are included in nonhuman resources like parks, library, shopping and recreational facilities. The non human resources are directly controlled or utilized by the human being.

The first step in management is to identify the various resources, and classify them and decide which resources are human and non human. This will help to decide what additional resources are needed and not available readily. It is important to recognize and use all kinds of resources are fully in achievement of the goals. The success of management process depends upon the recognition, allocation and use of resources.

The resources can also be classified as economic resource and non economic resources based on the monetary value they have or they can be classified by their availability in the family subsystem in near and larger environment (Ref: Gross et al 1973)

Human resources	Examples	Nonhuman Resources	Examples
Time	An hour or a lifetime to be used in activities of the individual	Material goods	Food, An owned home, Equipment, Car, Clothing, Paper clips, Consumer goods, Property, Furnishings.
Energy	Energy needed for walking upstairs	Money	Savings, Wages, Income from Investments, Shares

Interests	In gardening, folk music, or food preparation	Space	Large rooms which make possible entertainment of large groups of people Storage space, House
Intelligence	Seeing cause- effect relationship	Power	Electricity, Fuels
Ability or skills	Ability to plan, Skill in clothing construction, Ability to conduct a meeting	Community facilities	Libraries, Parks,
Knowledge	Information needed in selecting a car, Understanding principles of management		
Attitudes	Willingness to accept change, Optimism		
Creativity	Coning fruit, vegetables, and a figurine for a centerpieces		
Awareness	Watching for new products on market, Sensitivity to problems		
Standing plans	Routine for getting family off in morning		

In the second method the resources can be classified into three categories.

Human resources:

Cognitive: It is the component of thinking using knowledge, setting and defining goals, making plans etc. e.g. intelligence quotient.

Psychomotor: It assesses the physical costs of work in terms of effects on all the systems of the body that function during work e.g. skills.

Temporal: It deals with one of the resources with which the family's goals are achieved e.g. time.

Affective: It concerns the part that personal interests and attitudes play in making the work easy or difficult e.g. values.

Economic Resources:

Money Income: They are monetary benefit or gain derived from capital or labour e.g. salary.

Fringe Benefits: These resources are advantages in goods and services derived as a consequence of employment but exclude money income e.g. paid vacations.

Credit/Elastic Income: It is the current purchasing power expanded through deferred payments e.g. loans.

Wealth: It is a composite of holdings, real property and other income producing assets e.g. household durables, equipment, possessions etc.

Environment Resources:
1. Physical: Physical environment includes
2. Natural tangible environment - e.g. soil.
3. Natural non-tangible environment - e.g. air.
4. Social: These resources include
5. Social organisations - e.g NGO's.
6. Economic institutions - e.g. banks.
7. Political institutions - e.g. political parties.
8. Community .facilities - e.g. public utilities

The third method of classification is based on their economic value or worth, where in all resources are classified into two broad categories.

Economic Resources: These are those resources, which are utilised for production e.g. preparing meals for the generation of income (production).

Non-economic Resources: These are those resources, which are for self consumption e.g. preparing meals the family (self-consumption).

The fourth type of classification of resources is dependent on their tangibility or perception by touch.

Tangible Resources: These resources can be perceived by touch e.g. money.

Non-tangible Resources: These resources can not be perceived by touch e.g. skills.

Personal, Family, Community, National and World Resources

The fifth classification of resources is based on the social linkages of the organisation to which these resources belong.

Thus, resources are broadly divided into the following five categories.

Personal Resources: They belong to one individual e.g. skill.

Family Resources: They belong to the entire family members e.g. house.

Community Resources: They are available to the community from the neighbourhood e.g. banks

National Resources: These are available in the nation and the whole population is provided with these resources e.g. coal.

World Resources: These are shared by the entire population of the world e.g. services of the international organisations like WHO.

Family System and Household, Near and Larger Environment Resources

The sixth classification of resources is based on ecological approach, stressing upon the interrelationship between people and their environment where these resources are found. Thus, resources are divided into the following three categories.

Family System and Household Environment: These are resources available within the household environment, surrounding the family e.g. house, equipment, private transport etc.

Near Environment: It includes markets, educational facilities, recreational groups, medical facilities etc.

Human, Physical and Psychic Capital Resources

The seventh classification of resources is based on consumption economics. In this classification all resources are divided into the following three categories.

Human Capital: They include technology, capacity, motivation and time.

Physical Capital: They include the frequency and amount of income as well as purchasing power, elastic income, wealth and community facilities.

Psychic Capital: It is the degree of satisfaction derived from the expenditure of human and physical capital. It regulates the amount and quality of other resources required in the pursuit of satisfaction by all family members.

Renewable and Non-renewable Resources

The **eighth classification of resources** is based on their supply. In this classification natural shared resources are divided into the following two categories.

Renewable Resources: They include all those resources which can be replaced endlessly i.e. there is an endless supply. e.g. sun, wind, water, geo thermal.

Non-renewable Resources: They include all those resources which can be replaced tip to a limited period, after which its supply runs out. E.g. fossil fuels, wood etc.

Human, Non-human and Shared Resources

After studying all the above classification, a comprehensive classification is evolved, and suggested in this book, keeping in mind the resources available to an Indian family. This classification has three categories, human, non-human and community shared resources as can be seen from the following figure

2.3   Role of Resources in Management

Resources are very important in management of any institution or activity. Resources have three important roles.

- **Capacity to Meet Goals**:

  Resources have the potential to achieve targets. If we possess money but cannot use it to satisfy our needs, it cannot be termed as a resource. Resource is only that object or capacity that is available to be used for meeting our goals.

- **They can be Developed or Generated**:

  Certain resources like human resources, which include knowledge and skills, can be developed. It is also possible to generate material resources like money income, assets etc. with the help of human resource and visa versa. Thus, with efforts we can generate more resources or develop new ones. Development and generation of resources help us in meeting more goals and give us a power to determine the future and feeling of security and satisfaction. For example, a woman has developed a talent of making useful items from the waste material. She can use this talent for decorating her house or can also generate money by selling those items.

- **Resources can be Conserved or Saved for Future Use**:

Certain resources like money and material resources can be saved, for their use in future. Thus, they act as reservoir for meeting not only present but also future goals. It is also possible to conserve those resources, which might deplete soon and may not be available in future for use like oil reserves etc.

2.4 Characteristics of Resources

All the resources have three basic characteristics as identified by the senior management specialist. But in each case one must have information available about the potential of all available resources to be able to tap them effectively. Then only one could be able to conserve and judiciously use the resources. There are three important characteristics of all resources.

i. All resources are useful:

The definition of resource itself is indicative of this character. All resource have utility, which means they have the want satisfying power. The value or usefulness of any given element is recognized in relation to a specific goal.

Example: Money may be most valuable resources while purchasing a commodity. It may be a useless resource to pass an examination.

ii. Resources are limited:

All resources are scarce and some are scarcer. If all resources were in abundance, management would have been unnecessary. The challenge for management lies in the scarcity of resources and still being able to achieve the goal. The limits of each resource must be assessed in relation to the specific goals to be achieved. The limitation on the resources may be both quantitative and qualitative. The quantitative limitations can be accurate

Ex: time, money etc.

Though the resources like energy, intelligence can be quantified they cannot be assessed as measurable resources. Money can differ from other resources, which means that it is limited, but at the same time it can be procured through the investment of human resource. The quality differences in resources cannot be measured, but can be easily identified.

iii. All resources are interrelated:

People often may have to use a 'resource mix' or combination of different resources to achieve the family goals. This combination or mix of resources differs from individual to individual and family to family. Decisions cannot be taken up with use of one or two resources among the several available resources in isolation to achieve the goals. But by simultaneous usage of all the resources available (Ex: time and energy) the goals can be achieved. Hence use of resources is always an interrelated process. It is the integration of all the required resources, which is an important step in determining whether or not a goal will be attained. However, in identification of resources, alternatives can be worked out to be able to substitute or replace any resource if the need arises.

iv.   Resources are Accessible:

Resources are those assets, which are accessible for use. Skills of children become family resource only when children are available to help the homemaker. Resources are accessible in varying qualities or quantities. Some are easy to measure and others are difficult. Accessibility of material resources is easy to measure but some other human resources, though accessible, are difficult to measure. For example if a friend goes to the college in a car and gives another friend lift regularly, even friend's car can be considered resource. On the other hand, emotional support and courage are difficult to access, unless demanded though always they are part of human beings.

v.   Resources are Interchangeable:

All resources to a certain extent can be substituted for or interchanged with another resource. In the cases of their scarce availability, or simply for saving money, time, energy or environment, one resource can be used in the place of the other. A material resource can be interchanged with another material resource to save money or energy or even environment. For example if the cost of coffee beans goes up, it can be substituted with tea leaves to save that extra money spent on buying coffee.

A material resource can also be substituted by human resource in case latter is scarce or vice versa. For example if a home manager has little time or energy resource to do household work but has the money resource, she can hire paid help to do the work thus exchanging material (money) resource for human (energy) resource. Reversing the use of these two resources in another situation is also possible. For example, if a' home manager has the talent of being a good cook, she can earn material (money) resource in exchange of her human (energy) resource by supplying food for sale. Therefore, it is seen that it is possible to interchange one resource for another resource depending upon their availability, need and situation.

vi.   Management Process can be applied to all Resources:

In general, families need to be aware of the potential availability of resources within the family. Sometimes a homemaker may fail to recognise the human resource available in the family which could be utilized instead of using only the scarce resources like money, her time or energy. Lack of resources may make them feel uncomfortable and poor.

By management we have to narrow this gap by:

* Getting more resources

- Making our resources more productive and
- Changing our standards

All resources are manageable to some extent. Their quantity, quality, flow and their use can be regulated to certain degree. Thoughtful planning, organisation, control and evaluation can help a person in selecting the right resource at the time when that resource is in most demand and when it can get the best results. For example, careful choice of savings and investments for the higher education of one's child require a long term planning on how and how much money should be saved every month, besides organising the family efforts, control of money expenditure and evaluation of their activities. All these efforts will ultimately ensure that there are enough funds to cover for higher education. The task of saving money cannot be achieved by a homemaker without the understanding of process of management.

vii.   Quality of Life is determined by the Use of Resource:

It is clear that goals can be achieved only through the use of resources and their management. Therefore, the optimum distribution of resources determines the degree to which a family is actually striving towards a particular goal. Maintaining the health of the family members could be done by proper utilization of money and food resources according to the nutritional requirements of the family members. Time, energy and knowledge are also necessary to fulfill these goals.

Proper utilization of material resources like household equipments can lead to better products in food, clothing and house sanitation which are its contributors to better quality of life. Acquiring knowledge and its proper utilization can help one to make decisions for better quality of life.

2.5   Guidelines to Increase Satisfaction through Appropriate Use of Resources

The main objective of management of resources is to get maximum satisfaction from their use. Hoyt has given four guidlines for achieving maximum satisfaction.

- **Increasing the supply of resources:**

In order to increase the available resources, the family must ascertain its limits and see what is lacking in the total resource mix. This is called identification of resource gap. The resource gap can be identified by identifying where we want to be and where we actually are.

Ex: Increase in the time availability for a particular activity by hiring labor for other activities.

Increase in money income can be achieved by taking up employment or business during off time.

- **Knowing alternative use of resources:**

The alternate use of the given resource should be identified. The alternative use of time for various purposes could be identified and worked out in various management situations. One should ascertain the returns in terms of satisfaction from each of these alternative uses of resources. The possibility of alternative use of resources often allows the substitution of one resource for another which is scarce.

Ex: A women employed may have very little time for house work and spends money to hire a maid servant.

Increasing the utility and expanding appreciation:

All resources has alternate uses, but some specific goods have many possible uses. The selection of such a goods increase the utility.

Ex: sofa cum bed.

A home maker who opts for a sofa cum bed in a small flat can use it for sitting, sleeping and even storage purposes. Satisfaction increases if one finds new uses or combination of uses for things already owned. The use of multipurpose, space tools etc. could be of great help in increasing the utility.

- **Balancing the choice among the resources:**

In management it is important to represent the essential resources in good and correct proportion. For all individuals there should be some balance among interests, which would provide satisfaction. Work alone and play alone would not make life interesting and satisfying. In achieving balance of choices among alternatives, one must have representation of interests concerning individuals, family and the community, which could be of varying proportions. Hoyt was the author who listed six basic cultural interests which determine one's consumption of goods and services.

- Sensory: physical demands of the individual
- Social: desire for associating with people
- Intellectual: Creation of ideas
- Technological: carrying out the ideas
- Aesthetics: Importance of beauty
- Empathetic: relationships among family and society.

2.6   Conservation of Resources

Since the resources are limited, they have to be used carefully and conserved for future use. Some of the important points to be considered for conservation of resources are:

Resource Consciousness:

It means being aware and alert about resources. Sometimes we are not conscious about our resources, like human resource, which include the talents, skills etc. of the family members and shared resources like pure drinking water, clean and pure air, green cover etc. Being conscious about all the resources directs consciously 'and unconsciously our activities towards their conservation.

Adequate Supply

Ensuring adequate supply of resources also helps in conservation of resources. This is true especially in the case of larger family with lesser income. Such a family should make adequate efforts to supplement their income in a number of ways. Similar efforts should be made in the cases of other resources, especially shared ones which are in short supply like fuels for cooking & land for housing etc.

Use More of Abundant Resource to Conserve Scarce Resources:

The resources, which are available in abundance, should be used more than the scarce resources. For example a family which has many adult members and thus lot of energy available but has less income, should distribute work among its members by using their human resources instead of hiring domestic paid help to do their household work. Also a family can use solar energy, which is free of cost, available in abundance for cooking rather than spending non renewable and scarce fuels like coal, wood or LPG, and saving money simultaneously.

Avoiding Wastage:

Resources help in reaching goals, therefore, should never be wasted. A homemaker can use her extra time, energy and talents for productive work rather than waste it in idle gossip. Another very important example is avoiding the wastage of drinking water or electricity, which can be done in a number of ways. Close the taps properly when not in use, fill the bucket before bathing rather than using shower water to avoid wastage. Switching off the lights and fans of the rooms where no one is sitting, all the family members spending time together in one room so that the wastage of electricity can be avoided.

Economical Use of Resources:

Whether money or human resources, a family should use all its resources economically. Usually people are careful regarding their money and material resources, which are tangible and more easily recognized but forget the same for human resource. The time and energy of family members, fuels for cooking and transport, portable water, electricity etc. should also be used economically, so that their utility increases.

Resource Sharing:

Resources can also be conserved by sharing them. For example, car pooling or making use of public transport saves lot of petrol. Similarly work can also be shared. In a joint family, where there are more number of people, can share their household work thereby saving a lot of resources.

Managing Resources Wisely:

We have already discussed that resources can be managed and wise management can help in conservation of resources to a large extent. In the present times of resource crisis and shortage, applying managerial process in the use of every resource is very important.

Development and Use of Technology:

Development of such technology, which spares scarce resource by using less of scarce ones, can help in conserving resources. For example, developing technology to enable extensive use of solar energy, biogas and wind energy as domestic fuel or, for heating water or even for running vehicles will enable its use for these purposes possible. At present many of the technical advances are based on resource conservation, and the families should also make efforts towards this goal.

Recycling and Reuse of Resources:

Recycling of waste and reuse of certain resources is possible. Reusing paper can help in conserving forest by reducing the demand of wood for paper. Many of the household wastes like water garbage etc can easily be re-cycled and re-used for purposes like watering garden plants, biogas etc.

Making Wise Choices:

Making choices or taking wise decisions regarding the use of the resources available can also help in conserving them. This factor has been well discussed under the head, maximizing satisfaction in the use of resources.

2.7   Factors Affecting the Resource Use

Premavathy et,al have identified ten important factors influencing the use of resources:

1. Size of Income:

Money is a very versatile resource. This resource has a number of alternate uses. It can be exchanged for non-human resources suc as material goods and also for human resources such as skill, time, energy, etc. The size of income is correlated with the purchasing practices with decisions such as to when clothing and furnishing should be discarded, with the amount of paid help available to the homemaker, and with the presence of facilities and equipment in the home. When the size of income is more, there is a possibility that the family will be able to attain more' number of these goals. Larger the money income, higher will be the satisfaction of the family members. While the size of income affects the use of all resources, most of the information available on-this resource stresses the effect of income size upon its distribution oil the family needs.

2. Socio-Economic Status:

Social status indicates. a perceived relationship of a person to the social group. Social status accounts for differences in family values, attitudes, decision making and in expenditures pattern. In the modem urban areas, status is something which is achieved and not ascribed through birth. There is a social stratification in the society, as all people do not enjoy the same life style. An individual has many different positions in a society, each of which may have distinct status implications. Therefore, the individual's status is a composite of these different and sometimes contrasting aspects, rather than the result of anyone. These aspects and their interrelationships are constantly changing. The complexity of status determination demands great care in the selection if indices to status. Status groups are classified as upper-upper class, low-upper class, upper-middle class, lower-middle class, upper-lower class, and lower-lower class. Many families consciously or unconsciously, choose upward mobility as their goals. Upward mobility occurs only in terms of their education and occupation. To maintain a higher status, a family has to live up to it and this directly governs their expenditure pattern, values, goals and standards of status.

3. Occupation:

Traditionally the family's life-style, which include time schedule, the entertainment schedule etc. has been influenced by the husband's or the head of the family's occupation. The time schedule of the doctors and businessman's family differs from that of an ordinary middle income salaried family. The other factors such as the size of income, the status of the family, and their social circle, are also to a large extent determined by the occupation of the father. Traveling allowance, housing facilities etc. are all determined by the occupation, which again affects the status and the living styles of the family.

4. Gainful Employment of the Homemaker:

Women in the paid labour force affect resource allocation of all family members. Adding to a family income is considered one of the major reasons for married women for taking up gainful employment. The expenditure pattern also changes with the employment of women. Gainfully employed women use more purchased services, spend more on transport, clothes, labour saving devices, fast food etc.

5. Size and Composition of the Family:

The family size, age and sex make up the family composition that affects their resource usage. If a large family attends to maintain the same level of consumption as that of a small family, it is clear that it will require more commodities and services. Food, clothing, personal care, medical care and entertainment expenditures vary quiet directly with the size of the family while expenditures for equipment, housing and home furnishings are less variable as the size of the family changes.

The availability of the resources like time and energy for use increases as the size of the family increases. Similar to the size of the family, in the use of time, energy and other resources the composition of family assumes importance, If a large family is made up of adolescence and adults, more human resources are available' and extra demand on money resource may be expected. In a family where there is a grown up daughter, she may contribute to the availability of human resources by sharing the activities of her mother whereas a grown up boy may not be able to do so. Thus, the composition of the family in terms of sex affects the availability and use of their resources.

6. Motivation Attitude:

Motivation is an internal attitude. It is the way people use what they have that is important in meeting and establishing their goal. It directs or limits the quantity, quality, and the mixture of resources that a person is willing to use in goal attainment. When two children of the same family have two different attitudes, the one with increased motivation and positive attitudes than the other child, will do a better job as compared to the other. In a family where there is no motivation of family members with unfavorable attitudes towards the availability and use or resources, it is likely to affect the kind and number of goal achieved by them.

7. Education:

Formal education has direct influence on the amount of income earned. Person with increased education have more likelihood of earning better than others.

Women with more of formal education tend to take up gainful employment and so have less number of children thereby affecting the size of the family. Educated people have more geographic mobility, increased income and economic stability.

8. Family Heritage and Cultural Background:

This is an influential factor in transmitting family values. In our Indian society, we have joint family system in which grandparents, parents and children live together. The traditions, values, beliefs of the family are transmitted from older generation to the younger generation orally.

The cultural background of the family also affects the use of resources as the eating and spending, hobbies, their beliefs, festivals, superstitions etc. all are governed by this factor. This directly influences the way family utilizes its resources on various occasions or similar situations.

9. Location of the Family:

The location of a family within any community in relation to shopping areas, schools, place of husband's work and so forth will affect the homemaker's use of time, energy and other resources. Families living near the city, all the community facilities such as markets, schools, parks, dubs, banks, post office, etc. will be easily available to the family that may affect the use of resources such as time, energy and specially the money.

There is some marked difference in the use of their resources between the families in village area from the city families. Village families make up for an exchange of values because of the close, almost enforced association of families. In a city, families are so busy within themselves that they have no time for socialization or to think of culture. Whatever they, need, they buy them from tlle market. Similarly, families living a good shopping complex will have the tendency of spending more on clothes, eating out, shopping, etc. and so on. Nearness to or being away from the place of work or a school may affect the expenditure on transport or similar needs.

10. Health:

Health of all family members is important in home management. It is a state of complete physical, mental and social well being. Illness can make increased demand on managerial activities and resources such as money, time and energy. All such major resources are diverted when a family member's health is affected. A family, which enjoys good health, has an increased availability of resources to utilize or to meet more of their needs.

The efficient utilization of resources for attaining the family goals is influenced by the following factors according to Bharti and Jecintha(1994).

Family set up: The use of resources differ greatly with the size, set up, stage of family life cycle and the values, goals and standards of the family.

Surroundings and environment: Effective use of resources is also influenced by the social as well as natural environment.

Education of family members: If the family members are educated, the resources are utilized more efficiently and effectively. Lack of education may lead to wastage of resources.

Ex: time utilization.

Skill and abilities of the home maker: The use of family resources is affected to a maximum content by the skill and abilities of the house wife. A skillful and able home maker will use the resources more efficiently than the unskilled person.

Economic conditions of the family: Money is the most important resources both for attaining other resources as well as their usage.

Ex: use of soaps and detergents to wash cloths by a machine or a maid servant.

On management of resources, the essential thing to consider is the use of resources and not just the acquisition of goods, goals can be achieved only through the use of resources. Therefore the optimum distribution of resources determines the degree to which a family is actually striving towards a particular goal. Families should gear their management process towards achievement of short term and long term goals and increase the satisfaction of the family members.

References

1. Varghese, M. A., Ogale n. N. and Srinivasan K. 1985,
   Home Management, New Age International (P) Limited, Publishers New Delhi.
2. Irma H. Gross , Elizabeth Walbert Crandall and Marjorie M. Knoll,
   1973,Management for Modern Families (third edition) Prentice- Hall, Inc., Englewood Cliffs, New Jersey
3. Nickell, Paulena and Dorsey Jean M, 1970, Management in Family Living, New Delhi. Wiley Eastern Ltd.
4. DR. V.V. Bharathi and Ms. M Jacintha
   1994, Family Resource Management(New Concepts and Theory) Discovery Publishing House New Delhi.
5. Premavathy Seetharaman, Sonia Batra and Preeti Mehra 2005,
   An Introductionto Family Resource Management, CBS Publishers and Distributors, New Delhi
6. http://ecoursesonline.iasri.res.in/mod/page/view.php?id=28120

Chapter 3
The Management Process in Family Living Planning

Functions of Management: An overview
Management Process
a. Meaning and elements of process - planning, controlling the plan and evaluating, decision making
b. Planning - Importance, techniques, types of plan .
i. Controlling the plan in action
ii. Phases energizing checking - Factors in success of the control
Step – Suitability, Promptness - New decisions - Flexibility
iii. Supervisions of delegated plan - Types of supervision - direction and guidance - Analysis of supervision
iv. Evaluation - Importance, relationship to goals - Types-Informal and formal, overall and detailed - Techniques of self-evaluation - Evaluation of the whole process of management

Introduction

Management is a planned activity directed towards the realization of family values and satisfaction of wants of the family members. Management is a behavioral process that recognizes the actions and reactions of persons in living situations as they use the resources to achieve the desired goals. Home management is the purpose behavior involved in the creation and use of resources to achieve the family goals. Here effective use of resources becomes the focus of management.

Every individual or family does management, but some may be good managers and some may not be. But all manage with some degree of competence. The more skilled a person is in the process of management, the better will be the quality of living. Management is not only means to achieve the desired goals, but it is also a means to accomplish the self development, self actualization and renewal. Management consists of all behavioral processes experienced by people as they identify and cope with problems of setting goals, establishing and testing values and norms, identifying roles, solving conflicts, establishing power- authority lines within the family and influence patterns outside the family, perpetuating themselves and communicating with others in the solution of all these problems in their own particular situation.

Thus management is a process with a series of specific functions that bring about the desired results. The process provides an organised method of achieving the individual wants. The use of resources and the extent of achievement of family goals depend on the managerial interest, ability and leadership of each individual member of the family or group.

3.1 Planning

Planning is the beginning of the process of the management. Planning sets all other functions into action; it can be seen as the most basic function of management. Without planning other functions mere activity, producing nothing but chaos.

Planning is devising a scheme for reaching goals. It includes setting and clarify in goals establishing priorities among goals, establishing standards for measuring goals attainment and determining the activities needed to reach the goals. It includes a wide range of decisions dealing with family activities, resources and changing family wants. Planning is thinking through the possible ways of reaching a desire goal. They guide the persons or family is deciding what and how work or activities should be done and provides direction for utilizing resources throughout the management process. Planning includes setting standards to reconcile demands with resources and sequencing actions to meet the standards.

3.1.1 Importance of Planning

Terry defined planning as selecting and relating of facts and making and using assumptions regarding the future in visualization and formulation of proposed activity believed necessary to achieve desired result.

Gross and Crandall applied these definitions to home management and defined planning as specifying how family goals are to be reached. Thus, planning is a process by which a homemaker anticipates the future and discovers alternative courses of action open to her. She then consciously determines the future course of action to achieve the desired results by choosing a course of action from all available alternatives with the greatest economy and certainty.

It is essentially mapping out the courses of action to reach the goal. The need to develop a plan is derived from a felt need to resolve a problem or achieve something. The degree of satisfaction you attain will be dependent upon the completeness of the plan. In order to develop a workable plan one must identify and clarify the demand, event, problem or goal. The inputs during this stage include the values, standards and any information one has.

Although planning is always future oriented, plans vary in specificity from situation to situation. During the planning, standards are set which refers to the quantitative and qualitative measures of establishing standards depending on resource availability and other demands placed upon resources. The type of food served in the family is determined by the money available, the requirements of the people and the facilities and people available for the preparation. In purchasing furnishings for the home, the process of searching various furnishing materials involves the consideration of quality, cost, color, durability, and texture. Evaluation of the different alternatives in relation to the room to be furnished and the likes and dislikes of people inhabiting it, are other factors to be considered. Planning helps in a number of ways.

- **Planning helps to minimize risk and uncertainty:**

It helps the manager to cope with and prepare for the changing environment. It does not deal with future decisions, but with the futurity of present decisions. It is through planning the manager relates the uncertainties and possibilities of tomorrow to the facts of today and yesterday.

- **Planning leads to Success:**

Planning may not guarantee success but will definitely helps in directing towards the successful achievement of goals. It will help in shaping the environment which aid in successful achievement.

- **Planning focuses attention on the set goals:**

It plans the manager or the home maker to focus attention on the goals to be achieved and the activities need to be performed. It makes easier to apply and coordinate the resources more efficiently. It enables the manager to chalk-out in advances an orderly sequence of steps for the realization of the goals and avoids overlapping of the activities.

- **Planning facilities control:**

In planning, the manager sets goals and develops plans to accomplish these goals. These goals and plans then become standards or benchmarks against which performance can be measured. The function of control is to ensure that the activities conform to plans. Thus, controls can be exercised only if there are plans.

3.1.2 Characteristics of Planning

Planning as a function of management has certain characteristics. These characteristics help a homemaker in understanding the nature and purpose of planning in the management process.

I. **Privacy:** Planning is an important managerial function that usually precedes other functions. Thus it is a first step in the management process. However, it cannot be isolated from other managerial functions, which also have some impact on it.

II. **Contribution to Purpose and Objectives**: Planning contributes 1:0 the purposes and objectives of the management process. In planning, objectives are clearly stated by breaking the goal into smaller achievable targets.

III. **Intellectual Activity**: Planning is a mental activity. Rest of the management process involves its execution. Therefore, everything, which is needed to be done, is decided at the planning stage. Thus, it is not an action but an intellectual activity.

IV. **Continuity**: Planning is a continuous and never ending activity of a homemaker. When one goal is achieved, planning for the next goal starts, e.g. the first goal of the homemaker in the morning is to send children to school. After that, she starts planning for breakfast and then for lunch. Thus, planning is a continuous process. Even during the process of controlling some planning considerations are done to suit the changing situations and also during emergencies, when it calls for a modification in the original plan. Thus planning demands continuity.

V. **Flexibility:** Planning leads to the adoption of a specific course of action and the rejection of other possibilities. When the future cannot be moulded to conform to the course of action, the flexibility is to be imagined in planning by way of adopting the course of action according to the demands of current situations.

VI. **Unity**: Every family member makes his/her individual plans. Maintenance of consistency or unity of everyone's plans is an essential requirement of the planning of a homemaker. Therefore, whenever the homemaker plans, she should consider the individual plans of other family members and generate their consent to maintain unify in planning as well as in executing.

VII. **Precision:** Planning must be as precise as to its meaning, scope and nature. It should be framed in intelligible and meaningful terms by way of specifying the expected results. For example, the budget prepared by the homemaker for the family should be precise as far as possible so as to reach their goals conveniently.

VIII.   **Pervasiveness**: Planning is a pervasive activity covering the entire family and all aspect of family living. It is not the exclusive responsibility of homemaker alone. In the family each and every member should be directly involved while planning as it affects the future of every member and that of a family as a unit.

3.1.3 Types of Plans

The types of plans are viewed in terms of their uses and levels.

- **Use:**

Single use and repeat use or standing plans are in this category. Each will be considered with relation to the plans families may utilize. Single-use plans, as their name implies, are plans which are used only once. They may vary in any number of dimensions such as complexity or flexibility nevertheless, they are used only once. For example, the plan a family makes for a wedding reception is characterized by being attached to a goal which has a terminal point: the marriage of a family member. Some single-use plans tend to be rather large and detailed. The planners may exercise considerable care in developing them because they do not have the benefit of extensive past experience to guide them.

- **Repeat-use or standing plans:**

These are the plans that were designed to be used over and over again! The value of standing plans, according to Newman, is that they establish a pattern of action for "normal" situations so that the individual can then concentrate his attention on the changes he wishes to make in this' customary pattern of action for abnormal circumstances. A standing plan as conceived by Newman is similar to having a routine.

Successful routines, standing plans, or meta-plans require many conscious decisions when they are developed. They may be simple routines or fairly complex plans.

While single-use plans tend to have more alternatives attached to them, standing plans are in a constant state of revision due to their frequent use. Cumulatively, a large number of alternatives might be considered connection with frequently used plans, but the impact is not great at any one time.

- **Levels:**

Another way of classifying plans has to do with the general scope of the plan. Burk categorized planning as master planning, operational planning, and day-to-day planning. Master planning takes the form of establishment of goals, objectives, and broad policies. This level was discussed in the section on goal setting. Operational planning involves setting the standards and general procedures for running the various subsystems within the family. The third level, day-to-day planning, frequently is done almost unconsciously as general procedures are followed.

3.1.4 Techniques of Planning

Planning consists of a series of individual purposive decisions which follow a sequence or pattern. Each link is a series of actions performed so that a goal or objective can be reached.

For example: The family may have a goal of buying a new car. The goal will not be reached if the mother decides she wants a video set. In such cases, the chain is broken. There is no relationship between the goal of a new car and the impulse desire of a video set a saving programme and plans for a car trip would be more related.

There are five basic steps in planning. They are
1. Recognizing the problem
2. Seeing the different alternatives
3. Choosing between alternatives
4. Acting to carry out the plan
5. Accepting the consequences

In each problem, we have to analyze and clarify the situation to be able to define the problem. In view of the problem relevant alternatives are seen and analysed in relation to the pros and cons. Not all alternatives to our particular situation. The selection of relevant alternatives for solutions to problems is based on facts- not just on emotions and impulses. This means thinking through ideas, being conscious of people, family and others. This way, the choice is narrowed down to two or three alternatives. In selecting the best alternatives, one has to consider what will be given up if any one of these alternatives is selected. This has to be decided before making the final decision.
In planning, one has to essentially,

Balance between amount of available resources and the demands made upon it.
Ensure that the decisions made would be appropriate to the individual situations.
Make sure that plans are realistic and flexible.
If management is to achieve maximum satisfaction of living for a group, planning will be a group process. All persons who are affected by decisions and involved in group action need to be included in the planning and decision making process.

3.1.5 Dimensions of Planning

The important dimensions a plan as recognized by Gross, Crandall and Knoll are:

Complexity – occasioned by the number of parts within the plan and the interdependence of these parts.

Size-large activities frequently are termed molar while small activities are characterized as molecular. Presumably size could be associated with complexity since molar plans might be expected to have a larger number of parts than molecular plans.

Significance – in business and sometimes in family plans, significance may be determined by cost; anticipated income; anticipated effect upon members of the family or upon the employees; or the strategic nature of the plan in relation to the overall plan.

Comprehensiveness – in business comprehensiveness may be determined by the extent to which the plan cuts across departmental lines. In a family the extent to which family members are involved in or affected by the plan might be a criterion.

Time-frequently plans have been described as long-range or short-range. Tasker's and Mumaw's investigations covered short-range planning. i.e. daily or weekly plans. Dawson defined the shorter of her long-range plans as covering up to one year; the longer plans covered from two to ten years.

No general agreement has been found as to the length of time which could be considered long or short range. For business planning Le Breton suggested that time might be thought of in four parts: preparation time required for developing a plan; the lead time required for beginning work on major parts; the time required for full implementation; and the distance ahead one wishes to anticipate the future as a basis for general planning.

Specificity – the extent to which the parts of a plan are considered in general terms, on the one hand, or in definite, unequivocal terms, on the other.

Completeness-a complete plan includes all the necessary components for judgments to be made as to its acceptance or rejection or for its expeditious implementation.

Flexibility – refers to some parts of the plan which are fluid in nature or subject to change. Miller refers to a flexible plan as one in which the parts can be arranged in any order, for example, writing letters to five persons.

Extensity-number of plans generated over a specified period.

3.2   Organization

Organization is the logical arrangement of activities within a plan. It consists of dividing responsibilities among group members and delegating authority, scheduling and synchronizing the activities. In organization the responsibility is divided among the persons involved in complication of any task for achievement of any goal. The method of assessing task is turned as "task centered organization'. If task is assigned to a person for learning it, then that is called 'person centered organizations'.

Baker has given several levels of organizations which may be used in achieving goals. A level is one person organizing a task. Sometimes this is called work- simplifying. Another level is one person arranging his own efforts for the completion of several tasks he needs to do into a sequence or pattern. A mother employed outside her home is likely to be organized at this level. A third level is more complicated. It requires that the manager arrange the efforts of others who are doing the work into a pattern so that one or more tasks can be completed.

In performing the organizing function, the manager differentiates and integrates the activities of his organization. By differentiation is meant the process of departmentalization or segmentation of activities on the basis of some homogeneity. Integration is the process of achieving unity of effort among the various departments (segments or subsystems).

Gross and Grandell explains organisation as an orderly design a homemaker creates by planning and coordinating the activities of the home. They further stress that a homemaker has to organise the activities for self and for other as well.

Once the plan is ready, the required resources are sought in the step. Alternative resources or combination of resources, as per requirement of the plan will be brought together for attaining the desired goals. The responsibilities of various tasks in goal attainment will be delegated to the people involved in plan.

Organising also means that a homemaker coordinates the human and materialresources of   the family.   It   necessitates   that   she   must organise family members, materials, tasks and time. The effectiveness of an organisation depends on the ability of the homemaker to use family resources to attain its goals. Thus, during this process, proper relationship among work, people and other resources are established and the authority and responsibility are channelised. Therefore organising is an inseparable part of managerial action.

3.2.1 Importance of Organizing

Similar to planning, the homemaker should also understand why she must organize.

- **It Increases Management Efficiency**: Organisation increases the efficiency by avoiding delays and duplications. One task is assigned to only one person and every task is delegated so that no activity is left undone. This ensures efficiency in achieving family goals.

- **Optimum Use of Human Efforts**: Organising utilises the principle of specialisation. The tasks are assigned to the person who is the most capable of doing it. As we have discussed earlier that the housewife might allocate the responsibility of purchasing furniture to the husband who would be a better buyer for it while doing purchase of clothing herself as she can do it better than her husband, thus, making the best use of.human effort.

- **Laying Proportionate and Balanced Emphasis on Various Activities**: Organising ensures that due emphasis is given to each activity. Over emphasis on one activity.While ignoring or forgetting others should be avoided. For example, while organising, she may delegate the responsibility of dusting the house to the children, but she also has to ensure that they get enough time to study or can rather give some of her time to them to help them in their studies. Thus, she would be balancing between all the activities.

- **Facilitates Coordination**: Organisation helps in coordination of efforts of all· the members of the family. It also ensures the smooth flow of information and good communication among all the family members.

- **Provides Scope for Training and Development of Family Members:** Organisation has human focus rather than the work focus. People are given more importance than the actual work. Therefore, emphasis is on the development of skills, attitudes, capacities and creativity of the family members.

- **Helps to Consolidate Growth and Expenditure**: Organisation while regulating the expenditure of family income provides for the development of all the family members. Therefore, while achieving family goals, the whole family grows together as a unit.

- **Prevent Growth of Laggards, Wire pullers, Corrupters**: Organisation ensures that each member gives his or he contribution in the achievement of family goals, according to one's age and ability.

3.2.2 Characteristics of Organizing

Efficient organizing will contribute to the success of an enterprise and will have the following characteristics:

- It embodies the goals of the family.
- It helps to show the breakdown of goals.
- Helps each family member to see his tasks and resources he has to accomplish it. Tells each family member where his accountability lies and who are in his sphere of command.
- Family members know what communication to others is demanded of him and vise versa.
- Family members become aware of their rights and responsibilities.
- Helps vigilance against loss of resources and mis-direction, and reinforce economy and effort.
- Helps to secure the best out of the team of family members and adds the essential flexibility.
- Ensures work efficiency and order.
- Has human orientation rather than work orientation

3.2.3 Techniques of Organizing

The important techniques involved in organizing are

- **Identifying and Classifying Activities**:

Home maker must list all the activities which need to be done like buying groceries, vegetables etc., cooking meals, cleaning of the house, washing clothes and cleaning utensils.

- **Grouping Activities**:

Now all activities must be grouped the light of human and material resources available and the best way of using them.

- **Delegating Work:**

Each group of activities can be delegated to a person who can accomplish that work in the best possible manner. Each family member should also be assigned authority and resources necessary to perform these activities.

- **Delegation of Authority:**

This involves tying all the family members to either horizontally and vertically, through authority relationships and information flow

3.2.4 Coordination

Coordinating the efforts of all the family members is very important to achieve goals. Coordination helps to unify activities and parts of a plan into a harmonious and workable whole. It is necessary to coordinate the efforts of all individuals towards achieving common family objectives.

3.3 Implementation

Introduction

Implementing is putting the plan in to action. It is the accomplishment of goal through control of action, the evaluation of progress towards a goal and the adjustment of plans to meet the changing resources and needs. Implementing involves careful observation of the work performance. It is concerned with the cost in terms of resources like time, money, efforts and the satisfactions derived after the work or activity. Satisfaction can be so important in family living that a plan may be completely changed if one or more family members have negative feelings or are likely to be harmed in some way by the activities. Also, during implementing a goal may prove to be unwanted even though it had once seemed desirable because prediction is not always accurate. Thus implementing call for flexibility in thinking rather than a rigid pattern of action. Self discipline and supervision are very essential while implementing a plan.

Direction and guidance are the two aspects of supervision that parallel task and 'person centered' organization. Here it is very essential to have clear and instructions from effective implementation of the plan. Whenever safety is important in implementation of a plan accuracy of instruction is essential.

3.3.1 Characteristics of Implementation

The function of management involves the following activities:

Motivating and Guiding Personnel:- Homemaker has to motivate all the family members to work together to reach common family goals. It is for her to see that the morale of the members is high so that work is done quickly and efficiently.

Influencing and Shaping the Social System: Family is a smallest unit of society. Work patterns, which are developed at home, also influence the work outside home. Children learn the managerial abilities at home, which they utilize while doing every task throughout their life.

Understanding Followers and Securing their Cooperation: The homemaker has to understand the needs and capabilities, strengths and weaknesses, and problems of family members. This will help her in getting their cooperation in completing their assigned work and contributing in the familygoals.

Creating Climate for Performance: A positive and happy environment conducive for working with efficiency should be created by a homemaker.

Directing Efforts towards Defined Objectives: A homemaker must influence family members so that they will work willingly and enthusiastically towards the achievement of family goals.

To Get Full Co-operation from the Members: This function of management is very concrete, unlike planning and organisation, as it involves working directly with every family member. Homemaker should ensure that she gets full cooperation from family members at work.

3.3.2 Supervision is an important aspect of the process of implementation

The home manager along with working herself, she delegates work or tasks to the family members. She has to supervise the actual performance of the work, so that it will enable her to know whether the work is progressing in the right direction. Depending upon the situation she may have to guide, explain, instruct or demonstrate the work.

3.3.3 Checking and Adjusting

Checking is the examination of actions, which may be carried out by the planner or by the person or machine implementing the plan. When clothes are brought to the dry cleaner, they are checked for spots and decorations that need special attention and for other potential problems. Then they are checked afterward for appearance, for missing buttons decorations, and so on.

Transferring the responsibility of checking is widely practiced in family, financial management. Withholding from paychecks provides a way to control plans, whether the money is withheld for taxes, for united giving, for retirement, for health or automobile insurance, for stock-option plans, or for savings bonds.

Checking on a variety of factors has been reported in observations of grocery shopping. The process of selecting packages involves, "putting them down, fondling them, reading them, dropping them, picking them up and putting them back in the wrong place, etc.," and people sometimes look at weight, price, and what premiums are offered and read the fine print.

Adjusting is changing a planned standard, a sequence, or their underlying processes to increase the chances of the desired output. When there is deviation from planned behavior, as identified through checking, plans must be adjusted. If checking reveals a discrepancy between what is desired and what is being accomplished, adjusting takes place.

Facilitating:

Facilitating is assisting the progress or flow of actions by capitalizing on individual and/or environmental potential. Plans may include facilitating actions, and facilitating may originate while the plan is being implemented. The individual potential relates to the planners themselves and the environmental potential involves other persons and things in the situation. Conditions that promote achieving the standards or sequences of plans facilitate their implementation.

Facilitating processes may be evolved in the implementing subsystem. While implementing a task, a person may intuitively see an easier way to do the task, allowing the work to flow more continuously or more smoothly.

3.3.4 Benefits of Controlling

Some of the important benefits of the controlling process are:

- Ensures Performance According to Pre-determined Standards and Goal.
- Rescues and Provide Ways and Means for the Information Flow.
- It improves efficiency by saving time, money and energy.
- It aids coordination among all activities by regulating them.
- It helps in forward looking to achieve goals.
- It leads to greater organizational effectiveness by contributing to the achievement of goals.

3.3.5 Techniques of Controlling

They are those methods, which help in detecting the deviation in the performance. Primarily there are two types of methods. These are

I. **Budgetary**

II. **Non budgetary**

I. Budgetary Methods: These methods involve statement of anticipated results in numerical terms. Under this category the most important techniques, which can be used by the homemaker to control her plans are following:

Income and Expenditure Budget: This type of budget shows the family income from various sources and its distribution on family expenditure on various items for a specified period of time.

Cash Budget: This type of budget shows how much cash is available for expenditure and how much is already being consumed.

II. Non Budgetary Methods: These methods do not involve numeric but help in checking the activities necessary for achieving goals. Some of the most useful such techniques are following.

Mental Checklists: Most often homemakers prepare a checklist and mentally check, which activities are done and which are left. However, there is always a chance that she may forget one or more vital items of the checklist. But it is used most often and is quick and inexpensive way of checking especially when the activities are routine and not very important.

Records: This is a written form of checklist in which jobs, activities and even expenditure is recorded on a sheet of paper. The jobs completed are entered in the record and thus, a homemaker can assess the performance just by looking at a record. This method eliminates the error in checking due to forget but needs more time, energy and attitude of homemaker for writing the records.

3.3.6 Process of Controlling

The different phases of the control step are- energizing, checking and adjusting. The phase of 'energizing or initiating and sustaining the action' is very important in management. When the plans are made, many times we find there is inertia to get started especially if it is a big problem.

Here, the 'energizing' function would act as a catalyst. The creation of short-term objectives has several advantages to make the long term goals tangible and meaningful.

Example: graduation education only up to considering it year by year.

The second phase of controlling the plan action is 'checking' the progress of the plan. It is a quick step by step appraisal of a plan in action. For every household activity, one needs to time it so that all would be accomplished. Specific ways of checking plans in action vary with the resources concerned and the people involved in the process.

The third phase of 'control' step is 'adjusting' the plan if necessary. Situation might have changed which necessitates fresh decisions taking into account the problem in hand and the availability of resources. Essentially the control step is meant for making the plan work with individual or joint effort. It calls for guiding and directing self or others to carry through the plan.

3.4   Evaluating

Introduction

Evaluation is the final stage of management process. It consists of looking back over the steps of planning, organising, implementing and controlling to determine as accurately as possible, how good a Job has been done. Evaluating is assessing the progress in management subsystem and in goal attainment. The main functions of evaluation are assessing the impact of management and quality of living across time and consideration of possible improvement in the management processes. It is analyzing the results and judging the effectiveness of the plan. It helps to understand the reasons why outcomes are different from the desired goals. In managing family living the reasons why outcomes are different from the desired goals in managing family living, the measure by which relative success or failure of a plan can be evaluated is the extent to which it has the advanced the family goals. The more definite and clear cut the goals, the more accurate evolution can be alone.

Evaluating, as a distinct phase of management, goes beyond checking; it analyzes results and judges effectiveness. It attempts to discover reasons why outcomes vary from the projected or desired goal. It is a broader, longer view that analyzes impacts of action on the total pattern of living. Although evaluation centers on the outcome, it has many functions. In addition to analyzing the outcome, it provides information that can be used as a guideline.

Checking on management effectiveness or efficiency requires analysis, honesty, objectivity and a sound basis for judgment. In managing family living, the measure by which relative success or failure of a plan can be evaluated is the extent to which it has advanced the family's goals. The more definite and clear-cut the goals, the more accurate evaluation can be.

The positive or negative feedback promotes either continuity or change in the system. Positive feedback, reveals differences between expected and actual outcomes, acknowledges factors that support the deviation and favours an increase in or continuation of the deviation which is really a change in goal.

Negative feedback reveals differences between actual and devised output and influences the system to reduce the deviation so that the output stays within the established by goals or adjectives set.

3.4.1 Purpose of Evaluation

Lewin sees four purposes in evaluation and its purpose indicates its charactcristics:

1) To see what has been achieved.
2) To serve as a basis for the next plan.
3) To serve as a basis for modifing the overall plan, and
4) To gain new general insight.

Management Process Applied To Home Making Activities:

All functions of management process are closely interrelated. But to understand the process of management it is essential to analyze each function separately. Depending upon the goal to be achieved these functions may be analysed jointly or separately. Every home maker as a manager performs the following five basic managerial functions.

Formulated the objectives and the course of action to achieve the desired objective i.e. plan.

Establishes the structures, the system and the procedures to operation to achieve the objectives i.e organize.

Make the men, machine and methods in proper positions for accomplishing the overall objective and then implement and transmit the plan into actual action i.e co-ordinate and lead.

Check and make corrections as and when required as the plan is an action to bring performance in time with the actual plan i.e. control.

Review and evaluate the complete plan and the control measures applied to determine success or failure through its accomplishments and also to suggest methods of improvement in future planning and controlling measures i.e. evaluation.

The major managerial responsibility in family consists of the following.

1) Identifying values and selecting goal.
2) Create healthy environment in home and community.
3) Achieve desirable inter personal relationships.
4) Nurture growth and development of the young.
5) Plan of work for long range financial security.
6) Maintaining a pleasant and comfortable home.
7) Providing suitable food and clothing for the family.
8) Purchase consumer goods and services.
9) Maintaining the health of all family members.
10) Perform tasks of maintaining the home, using time and energy wisely.
11) Guiding educational and social developments of the individual in the family group.

Participate intelligently in community, legislative and social action affairs.

Thus effective management requires the understanding and implementation of the principles and process involved. It is clear that a homemaker can be successful only when she practices them properly along with the co-operation of all the family members concerned.

References

1) Varghese, M. A., Ogale n. N. and Srinivasan K. 1985, Home Management, New Age International (P) Limited, Publishers New Delhi

2) Irma H. Gross , Elizabeth Walbert Crandall and Marjorie M. Knoll, 1973,Management for Modern Families (third edition) Prentice- Hall, Inc., Englewood Cliffs, New Jersey

3) Nickell, Paulena and Dorsey Jean M, 1970, Management in Family Living, New Delhi. Wiley Eastern Ltd.

4) DR. V.V.Bharathi and Ms. M Jacintha 1994, Family Resource Management (New Concepts and Theory) Discovery Publishing House New Delhi.

5) P.C Tripathi and P.N Reddy 1983, Principles of Management (Third Edition), Tata McGraw-Hill Publishing Company Limited, New Delhi.

6) Premavathy Seetharaman, Sonia Batra and Preeti Mehra 2005, An Introduction toFamily Resource Management, CBS Publishers and Distributors, New Delhi

7) Ruth E Deacon and Francille M. Firebaugh 1975, Home Management Context and Concepts, Houghton Mifflin Company, New Jersey

8) http://ecoursesonline.iasri.res.in/mod/page/view.php?id=28325

9) http://www.familyresourcemanagement.org/services/management/

Chapter 4
Management of Time in Family Living

Management of specific Family Resources:
Time management – Step of making time plan, factors affecting time plan, leisure time activities.
Time demands in family life cycle, Time norms & pattern of time use

4.1   Time Management

As a resource, time can be used in several ways. It is combined with other resources to achieve a desired goal or meet a demand. Within the management process we make decisions concerning its use. It may be allocated for transferring, exchanging, producing, protecting, saving-investing, or consuming.

Using time effectively calls upon your knowledge of the quantitative and qualitative aspects of any other resources combined with your time resource. In addition to this, it also necessitates examining available resources and determining which combination of resources will bring about the greatest degree of satisfaction while minimizing the use of each. It means examining time resources along with all the others.

- Effective time management involves the following:
- Recognizing the demands placed upon your time.
- Ascertaining the goals which necessitate the use of your time resources.
- Identifying and setting priorities for these demands and goals.
- Determining which resources to combine with your time resource to enable you to meet demands and achieve goals.
- Recognizing those demands which cannot be altered or changed.
- Identifying any constraints upon both your time and other resources.
- Developing a plan to allocate and use your time resources.

4.1.1 Time Demands in Stages of Family Life Cycle

The time demands change according to different stages of family life cycle. A family in the beginning stage with only two partners may have lesser time demands for the home maker. As the family size increases with the coming of children time management becomes most essential as she will be pressurized with lots of time demands for various activities. During the contracting stage of family life cycle the time demands of the home maker starts decreasing.

Understanding the demands on the homemaker's time during the different stages of the family life cycle will help families plan ahead and prepare themselves to meet new and changing time demands.

Stage I: The beginning family is a period of adjustment and child bearing for young homemakers. At this stage, family goals, time and work patterns, work habits, and the division of responsibilities between husband and wife are established. Unless the homemaker is employed outside the home, demands on her time are light.

Stage II: The expanding family brings new and heavy demands on both the parents. The coming of children requires the greatest adjustment in the time patterns of homemakers. Farm and city homemakers with children under a year old used from twenty one to twenty five hours a week in caring for their families according to some studies. They used about thirteen hours when the youngest child was one to two years old. Thereafter their time demands decreased steadily until the youngest child was about nine years old. While children are in grade school and high school, their time demands, although different, remain high. They center around the problems of guiding and directing children in assuming their places as responsible members of the family, of making time plans together and helping each one to evaluate their use of time. As children approach and reach adulthood, demands on the homemakers time depend on whether the children go to college, marriage and leave home, or whether they take jobs and live at home.

Stage III: The contracting family covers the period during which the children have become independent. Mothers now have some free time to use as they wish. They can make the most of these years by learning to co-ordinate their time and recreation plans with those of their husbands. The curve in figure shows that the time demands upon the homemaker rise rapidly with the coming of children and remain high until the children complete their education and leave home. A gradual drop comes with the approach of the retirement period.

Managing the time involves both making the plan and carrying them out. A time plan shows what one expects to do in a given period of time. While making the time plan one has to think about the problems in advance, which can be prevented through careful planning. A time plan indicates the sequence of activities. To make an efficient, workable plan each home maker, with the help of her family members should decide what activities are to be carried out daily, weekly what season the task should be planed etc.

4.1.2 Pattern of Time Use and Time Norms

As average home maker spends her time in various activities such as food preparation, dish washing, maintenance of home, care of family members, shopping, education of children, social and religious activities and managerial activities.

The pattern of time use is classified into two groups:

Work time and Leisure time.

- **Work time**:

Work is defined as activities producing measurable results for one's self or others. The varieties of work time include time used for pay, household or home-related work, and volunteer work.

- **Employment:**

Time devoted to employment for pay is one category of work time. Employment time differs with the specific job. The specific nature of work hours influences the duration of non work activities and also affects synchronization of personal activities with those of others.

- **Home-related work:**

Household care, personal care and care of other family members is another form of productive or work time. Although the time requirements of specific household work have changed with the technological advancement, the average requirement of time is almost same.

- **Volunteer work:**

Time contributed to the religious activities a community activities or a national activities for no monetary pay is termed volunteer time.Although people using time for community or household work art not often paid a wage, this time use does affect personal, household, community, and national quality of life.

- **Non-work time:**

Sleep is one of the most time-consuming of all human activities. It accounts for about one-third of an adult's day and an even larger share of a child! Day. Although sleep is needed for survival, the specific amount needed varies with each person. While one person may be refreshed after six hours of sleep others may need nine or more hours of sleep each day. In addition to sleep free time and leisure are classified as non-work time.

- **Free Time:**

Time not devoted to work or to sleep is called free time. Free time may imposed or may occur by choice. A person who seeks full time work but car find only a part-time job or cannot find work is faced with imposed free time If the man or woman has insufficient nonhuman, economic resources-mane transportation, or tools-or lacks interest in free-time activities, this time be a constraint rather than as a resource

Leisure time:

Time spent in activities chosen by the individual and rewarding for its own sake is leisure. In other words, leisure is un-imposed free time. Family picnics. Water-skiing, horse riding, tennis, reading, or other activities not related to work roles are also considered leisure-time activities.

The time use for specific roles and activities limit the choice available for other time uses. Time is an influential resource because it is used with other resources to reach the desired goals. Through application of management principles, individuals and families can utilize time to achieve desired quality of life.

4.1.3 Time Norms for Household Tasks

Some attempts have been made to establish norms or average times spent on specific household tasks such as bed- making, washing windows and so forth. Whether or not established norms exist and are known to the home-maker who wishes to manage her time, knowledge of her own time costs is extremely important. Over a period of years a home-maker probably knows about how long it takes her to complete most of her various repetitive tasks.

The study by Batra S. and Seetharaman P. (2000) also reported Time norms for various activities. These are as follows:

Homemaking Activities

The full time home-makers spent maximum time, 6.58 hours on homemaking activities followed by business class, 3.92 hours. The least amount of time was spent by service class, i.e. 3.05 hours on this activity in a day.

Employment Related Activities

The respondents from service class spent maximum amount of time, 6.63 hours on this activity followed by business class 6.54 hours and professional class 6.46 hours. The least amount of time, 5.04 hours was spent by academicians on employment related activities in day.

Personal Activities:

The respondents from Academic Class spent maximum amount of time 10.22 hours on personal activities followed by full time home-makers, 9.51 hours. The least amount of time, 8.26 hours was spent by professional class on personal activities in a day.

Miscellaneous Activities:

The full time home-makers spent maximum amount of time, 3.19 hours on miscellaneous activities followed by professional class, 2.46 hours and business class, 2.45 hours. The least amount of time, i.e. 2.21 hours was spent by service class on miscellaneous activities in a day.

Norms for Leisure Time:

Some norms are available for leisure time activities of home-makers, Leisure activities may be broadly interpreted as anything not classified as work or rest, and in this interpretation include such uses of time as eating and dressing. They may also be more rigidly interpreted. There is evidence that even in the most restricted sense; leisure is a fairly important part of a homemaker's day. The Weigh and study shows a daily average for full time home-makers of approximately 4 to 5 hours spent on community activities and other leisure time activities.

4.1.4 Tools of Time Management

There are various tools involved in the management of work time. It is very important to consider them while managing time. They provide the basis for time management. These are as follows:

- Peak Loads
- Work Curves
- Rest periods, and
- Work Simplification

1) Peak Loads:

This is one of the important tools to be considered while managing work time. For most people activities pile up on each other at certain times of the day or the week or the month or the season. These packed periods are called peak -loads. For example, for a homemaker peak loads can be daily, weekly or seasonal such as the time of breakfast and getting the family off for the day is a daily peak load, the thorough cleaning of the house a periodic peak load and the Diwali or a festival preparation, a seasonal peak load.

The peak load may be lessened by delegating some work to other family members or by adopting some work simplification methods. Awareness of the peak load and the methods of handling them is an important tool for managing time. This is even more important for a homemaker who is gainfully employed outside the home.

2) Work Curves:

The second tool for managing work time is the work curve. A typical work curve has the following features:

- Starts sluggishly
- Sharp rise as worker gets into stride
- Falling off in the middle of the spell with a fresh spurt as work nears its end
- Find falling at the last hour

In analysing a hypothetical work curve shown in the figure 31.1 with a lunch break, the preliminary increase, 'a-b' signifies the warming up period known as the 'warming up'. The letter 'b-c' indicate the plateau of greatest steady production 'e-d' shows the first major drop in production. Production starts out at a higher level after lunch than in the morning but never reaches as high as 'b-e' in the morning. The figure shows a decrease in production and that is due to the effect of accumulated fatigue at the end of the day. The worker may stop at, ' f ' or continue to' g,' but the production level will decrease from 'f' onwards. The drop from 'e - d' is supposedly due to boredom developing during the job if the work is light. In heavy manual labour the final decrease will probably be very great and it is possible that output may fall to zero if work is continued further to the point of exhaustion.

A most desirable work curve is done in which ab warming up (wu) is (a) steep line showing that worker got into the swing of work rapidly and (b) achieved a high plateau of production -longer the plateau of production, greater the output of work accomplished.

3) Rest Periods:

This is the third tool for time management. A rest period need not mean complete cessation from work, although that is desirable after a heavy manual labour. The greatest results can be expected if the worker lies down and relaxes completely, because reclining requires less expenditure of energy than any other body position. As compared to most workers, the homemaker can provide good conditions for rest more easily. A change in the type of work may also serve as rest periods for each other.

4) Work Simplification:

It is also one of the tools of time management which is related to energy management, as it includes improving methods of work which requires lowering both time and energy expenditures, because the time and energy are required to do any task and they largely depend on the hand and body motions used.

In simple terms, work simplification is the conscious seeking of the simplest, easiest, and quickest method of doing work. Or in other words we can say that work simplification means improvement in performance of task.

It is a very important tool of time management which not only is helpful in an industry but a very useful tool for a homemaker who wants to have a liberal supply of time as well as the need to conserve her energy.

4.1.5 Time Plan and Steps in Making Plan
4.1.5.1 Time Plans

Managing time involves both making plans and carrying them out. A time plan shows what one expects to do in a given period such as a morning, an afternoon, or possibly during a whole day or a week.

Most home-makers follow some sort of time plans. As might be expected, all do not manage time equally well. Some studies have shown that home managers tend to fall into three groups:

A small group for whom home work is a minor consideration.

A large group who by careful management fit most of their work into the morning and into an hour or two in the afternoon with many afternoon and evenings relatively free for the children, their husbands, social life and community activities.

A large group for whom each day is a nip-and-tuck race to accomplish the things that must be done between morning and bed time with occasional afternoons and evenings free only by planning for them well in advance.

The success or failure of these groups of homemakers is due largely to their approach to homemaking responsibilities. Homemaking and managerial skills can be learned if one is interested and willing to work and study.

4.1.5.2 Steps in Making Daily and Weekly Time and Activity Plans

A workable time and activity plan must be built step by step to fit the needs of one's family. Conditions in no two homes are the same. Plans for a family with young children will differ greatly from a family with teenage children. Some homemakers, such as doctors', and farmers' wives, must dovetail their work with that of their husbands and plan time for interruptions and unexpected demands, because they are a part of the day's activity. Although the details of time and activity plans will differ in each household, the steps in making them are much the same.

Step 1: Consists of listing the everyday, weekly, special and recreational activities of the family. The list will probably include such tasks as the follow

Every day Jobs and Activities

- Caring for children and invalids
- planning, preparing and serving meals
- Packing lunches
- Baking cookies, cakes, breads
- Preparing baby's food and caring for baby
- Washing dishes
- Doing unexpected tasks
- Making beds
- Caring for house
- Caring for pets
- Resting and personal care
- Recreation and social activities
- Doing farm work
- Doing any other tasks

Weekly and Special Tasks And Activities:

- Washing and ironing
- Mending and sewing
- Cleaning house thoroughly
- Other special cleaning
- Shopping and ordering
- Washing Windows
- Special cooking and baking
- Preparing special meals
- Going to meetings, clubs etc.
- Doing any other tasks
- Going to doctor, dentist etc.
- Errands away from home
- Doing farm tasks
- Making repairs on equipment and house
- Going to bank and keeping accounts
- Engaging in recreational activities.

Seasonal Tasks and Activities:

- Planning and directing children's vacation activities.
- Preparing for holidays
- Preparing for birthdays
- Storing seasonal clothing
- Preserving food
- Sewing
- Vegetable and flower gardening Caring for yard
- Putting on and taking off screens and storm windows
- Doing any other tasks.

Step 2: Consists of making a plan for everyday or routine tasks and starting or underlining those that must be done at a definite time. This provides a skeleton around which build the rest of the plans. Such duties as preparing and serving meals, packing up lunches, taking children to school and picking them up and daily cleaning are included in this skeleton plan.

Step 3: Consists of completing the weekly plan. At this point we must fit the weekly, special and seasonal jobs into the free blocks of time in the daily plan. In allocating these jobs the homemaker must consider the needs of her own household, the work habits and free time of members of the family.

Step 4: Consists of deciding who will do various tasks and calls for group discussion and planning. In doing this, the work carried out by the mother and father individually as well as the responsibilities they share together and the duties of each child, no matter how small, are clearly defined and understood. Step 4 is usually combined with steps 2 and 3, because many of these decisions are made when the order and time of work are being determined.

4.1.6 Time Schedules

Introduction

It is necessary for the home maker to prepare time schedules. It is very difficult to make a specific time schedule for each and every individual. Hence a general time schedule can be serving as a guide to making individual time schedules to every family member.

4.1.7 Types of Time Schedules

The time schedules may be daily schedule, weekly schedule and seasonal schedule for a home maker who is not employed outside. Among all the stages of family life cycle the highest demand on time is felt during the expanding stage of the family. Premavathy et al (2005) have given some sample time schedules of the home maker as reference for making individual time schedules. Daily time schedule for a housewife

From	To	Plan
5.30 am	6.00 am	Personal care like getting up, brushing, taking a cup of tea etc.
6.00 am	7.00 am	Prepare and pack breakfast for self, children and husband
7.00 am	7.45 am	Prepare and serve breakfast to the family members and self.
7.45 am	9.00 am	Clear table, supervise kitchen work as maid washes dishes, daily cleaning, straightening and bed making
9.00 am	10.00 am	Sorting and washing clothes by hand or machine, putting these clothes for drying etc., bathing and dressing.
(10.00) am	(11.30) am	Provision for weekly tasks and activities
11.30 am	12.00 noon	Rest and reading newspapers, magazines, watching television etc, or some leisure time hobby work like sewing embroidery etc.
12.00 noon	1.00 pm	Prepare lunch and semi preparation and planning for evening snacks and dinner
1.00 pm	1.30 pm	Watch TV or do some hobby work/resting
1.30 pm	1.45 pm	Bringing children back from school/bus stop.
1.45 pm	2.30 pm	Serve lunch to children and cleaning up

2.30 pm	3.30 pm	Rest and getting in touch with friends and relatives on telephone etc.
3.30 pm	5.00 pm	Help children with study and homework
5.00 pm	6.00 pm	Allow for weekly tasks and activities
6.00 pm	6.30 pm	Prepare, serve and have tea, snacks, with family members
6.30 pm	7.30 pm	Preparations for dinner
7.30 pm	8.00 pm	Help children pack bags, prepare for next day's activities.
8.00 pm	8.30 pm	Serve and have dinner with family members
8.30 pm	9.00 pm	Clear table, clean kitchen etc.
9.00 pm	10.00 pm	Spending time with family members/watching television etc.

Daily time schedule for a working woman

From	To	Plan
5.30 am	6.00 am	Personal care like getting up, brushing, having a cup of tea etc.
6.00 am	8.30 am	Preparing breakfast and lunch for family members
8.30 am	8.50 am	Having breakfast with family and cleaning
8.50 am	9.00 am	Getting ready for office
9.00 am	9.45 am	Going to office-Traveling
9.45 am	1.00 pm	Attending office work
1.00 pm.	2.00 pm	Lunch break
2.00 pm	5.30 pm	Attending office work
5.30 pm	6.15 pm	Going to home-traveling
6.15 pm	7.00 pm	Relaxation, Preparing and having snacks and tea.

7.00 pm	7.30 pm	Watching T.V. reading newspapers and magazines
7.30 pm	8.30 pm	Helping children in study
8.30 pm	9.15 pm	Preparing dinner for the family
9.15 pm	9.45 pm	Having dinner with family
9.45 pm	10.30 pm	Kitchen cleaning and next day preparation
10.30 pm	-	Going to bed

Weekly time schedule for a housewife (10.00-11.30 a.m.

DAY/DATE	Plan
Monday	computer classes
Tuesday	Mend and sew
Wednesday	Attend computer classes
Thursday	Interaction with friends, Recreation and social activities
Friday	Attend computer classes
Saturday	Shop for groceries and other items
Sunday	Spend time with family members at home or having an outing/visiting friends, relatives etc.
(2.30-6.30 p.m.)	
DAY/DATE	Plan
Monday	Drop children for tennis, music, dance or Hobby classes,
Tuesday	and go for walk.
Wednesday	Same schedule is followed.
Thursday	Same schedule is followed.
Friday	Same schedule is followed.
Saturday	Same schedule is followed.
*Sunday	Family outing or spending time together on indoor games. Spend time with family members at home or having an outing/visiting friends, relatives etc

* On Sundays no fixed time schedule is followed, there is flexibility in time plans according to the needs, desires and requirements of the family and friends
Table 32.4 Seasonal time Schedule for a housewife.

Season	Plan
Spring	Vegetable and flower gardening
Winter	Storing seasonal clothing and preparing the wardrobe for the next season.
Summer	Plan and prepare for holidays. Plan and direct activities for children during vacations. Preserving food - making pickles, chutneys etc., storing seasonal clothing
Monsoon	Vegetable and flower gardening

4.1.8 Steps in Preparation of a Time Schedule

Time schedule should be carried out through a set of a fairly definite steps which are as follows:

1. List all items to be Included, Grouping under Flexible and Inflexible.

In some cases, there is only a fine line separating flexible from inflexible items. For example, go~ to classes is inflexible for a student, or feeding the baby is inflexible for a home-maker, where as dusting one's bedroom or living room is a flexible task, which need not be done at a fixed time. It is equally important to break down lengthy or complicated tasks into parts. Not only are parts easier to grasp and to check on later, but they are easier to face and perform. Thus these activities are to be listed and arranged in a sequential order.

2. Set Down as Accurate an Estimate of Time for Each Task as is Obtainable.

Settings down of time estimates may be accomplished in one of two ways: Either the person uses her own time norms found through long experience or through keeping a few records of repetitive tasks or she must estimate as best she can, the time required for each part of her schedule, get such information from other sources such as friends, relatives or books. This time estimates are important, because the homemaker who takes two hours to clean a closet today should know that she cannot clean three closets in the same amount of time tomorrow or on any other day. Thus estimating the required time for each task is important, prior to the preparation of a final time schedule.

3. Bring Total Estimated Time Needed and Total Available Time into Harmony.

The third step in making a time schedule, bringing needs and wants into harmony, is the same process as that applied to the more tangible resource-money. This is done generally and felt more in the preparation of a budget in the financial management. This step calls for adjustment and listing the earlier activity of flexible and inflexible plays an important role here.

4. Determine Time Sequence.

It requires both listing jobs in order and determining logical times when they are to be done. Such as, build around the tasks that are fixed both as to necessity of performing them and/ or clock time when they must be done, alternate light and heavy jobs as far as possible, include elasticity periods without fail. Sequence of activities can be planned most effectively, if we take into consideration the aspects such as fixed jobs, regular, routine, rest periods and the warming up period. This step requires a lot of care, since one has to bring a good balance in the use of time resource.

5. Write out Plan.

Now check the above sequence of activities before preparing the actual final plan of action. If the period planned for is short enough and soon enough, so that all the preceding steps may be accomplished while the plan can be remembered. Forms for writing out time plans vary from a separate card for a day with a few notations to a week's or even a month's plan. It all depends upon the convenience of the person for whom the plan is made.

6. Merge Individual Plans with Others for Co-ordination.

The carrying out of the last step depends upon whether or not one is working alone. A homemaker may need especially to co-ordinate her plans with those of other family members, especially that of the adult members in the family, like her husband, grown up children, elderly parents etc.

4.1.9 Factors Influencing Time Use

The efficiency in using time is broadly based on the concept importance a person or family holds for it.

- **Economic and social states**: A person who high economic and social status is usually required to participate in the community welfare activities, social activities etc which demands proper time plan.
- **Education:** The education plays a major role in effective time plan and usage it is a known fact that an educated person understand the importance of time and can take better decision is time use.
- **Areas/Distance** the locality in which a person lines does have an impact in the use of time Example: Distance between residence and market educational institutions, job place etc.

- **Special interest and creative activities**: If a person is talented and interested in any creative activities he/she may not mind spending time for those activities that give satisfaction and relaxation to them.
- **Congenial conditions**: while playing any role either in home or outside a congenial, comfortable environment with innovative, simple, operating work simplification equipment will enable a housewife to use her time efficiently she can conserve time for other activities.
- **Health, age and sex:** A healthy young individual is generally energetic and his capacity is doing a job is faster when impaired to an old person though woman have equality right in par with men yet their potentials are not fully recognized in most of the families because of this she may face hurdles and stress in time management.
- **Family size**: size of the family is factors which affects the time spent in home making.
- **Division of labour:** When the family activities are shouldered by all members in the family the time burned is reduced on the homemaker.
- Management through tools: The philosophy of management is based on relegations of time availability and her attuned towards management knowledge of tome patterns of various household activities pattern of various household activities and her attitude towards management knowledge for time pattern of various house hold activities is an aid for effective time management time pattern can be obtained by observing daily records of makers time use Most of the Indian women spend more time in the kitchen and other house hold activities employed women usually take time to spare for their children.

References

1) Nickell, Paulena and Dorsey Jean M, 1970, Management in Family Living, New Delhi. Wiley Eastern Ltd.
2) Premavathy Seetharaman, Sonia Batra and Preeti Mehra 2005, An Introduction toFamily Resource Management, CBS Publishers and Distributors, New Delhi
3) Betty B. Swanson 1981, Introduction to Home Management, Macmillan publishing co., Inc. New York.
4) http://ecoursesonline.iasri.res.in/mod/page/view.php?id=28356

Chapter 5
Energy Management

Energy management – work simplification process, Types of fatigue and its reduction, Mundel's classes of change.

Introduction

Energy is the basic requirements of every person for maintenance of life, growth and physical output. Time can be planned and monitored according to the activity but it is not easy to plan and monitor the energy requirement as per the activity. It varies from person to person and is influenced by the physical and physiological body parameter. The energy is obtained through the dynamic biochemical reactions in the body and is utilized for

- Maintenance of basal metabolic process.
- Promoting growth.
- Regulation of body temperature.
- Performance of various physical activities

As a resource, energy is intangible. Evidences of its existence can be demonstrated by the tasks we accomplish, the activities we undertake, and the speed at which we complete tasks.

The major emphasis concerning resources is maximizing its utilization. Energy resource occurs in limited amounts and its management should be directed toward maximizing as much as possible the use of this valuable resource to ensure that you have enough energy remaining to meet your other demands. This necessitates becoming aware of our physical actions, and the effect of our attitudes upon this resource. Each of these plays an important role in energy utilization. Thus allocation and use should be directed toward conservation rather than consumption.

5.1 Energy in Different Stages of the Family Life Cycle

The energy demand of the home maker varies according to the stages of the family life cycle. Energy demands are usually lowest during Stage I, the beginning family stage. If the homemaker works outside the home, however, she must learn to divide her energy between the demands of her outside work and her home responsibilities. The busiest years for the homemaker occur during Stage II, the period during which the family is expanding. Young children require more care, and after the children start going to school, meeting all the family demands both inside and outside the home requires a great deal of energy.

When the children reach college age and begin to leave home, Stage III, the contracting stage, begins. As their energy loads lighten at home, many homemakers resume professional and outside interests. Helping married children, and welcoming new members to their families often brings additional responsibilities. During this stage, energy supply may diminish and physical disabilities may require the reshaping of energy spending patterns.

5.2 Energy Costs of Households and Occupational Activities

A combination of several types of efforts like manual effort, mental effort, visual effort, torsal effort and pedal efforts are needed to perform any activity. The energy costs change according to the combination of the types of efforts used for each activity. In order to have well balanced energy expenditure pattern, the home maker need to know the energy costs of various activities. The energy costs are calculated based on the oxygen consumption per minute or the heart rate (beats per minute) while performing the activity.

The household tasks mentioned in the various studies have been classified according to energy costs as light, moderate, and heavy, and are given in the following table. This covers a wide range of activities and includes many of the tasks most frequently done in the home. Moderate or heavy work requires walking and standing as well as different forms of manual and torsal effort. Checking the energy costs as given in the list against the different forms of the effort used in their performance will help the home-maker to select light, moderate, or heavy energy demanding tasks to make a comfortable daily and weekly work load.

Most Tiring activities:

Many homemakers indicated cleaning and caring for the house and washing and ironing tasks were most tiring and the tasks they disliked most.

In this fast world, where everyone wants to utilize even a second of his or her time and energy to convert them into money for his or her family's well-being, the use of both the resources time and energy are of very great importance. Clear understanding on how energy can be managed is of great importance, since time and energy are related resources, especially for the homemaker who has to go out for work, besides working in the house. Where ever more time is spent on a task, it also means a higher expenditure of energy resource.

5.3   Energy requirement for various activities

Light:1.4-2 Calories per minute	Moderate:2-3.5 Calories per minute	Heavy:3.5-4.5 Calories per Minute
Hemming	Using carpet sweeper	Scrubbing floor
Knitting	Using vacuum sweeper	Mopping floor
Crocheting	Polishing furniture	Waxing floor
Darning	Kneading dough	Taking out and hanging laundry
Hand sewing	Wringing clothes with electric wringer	Washing kitchen floor
Machine sewing machine	Hanging clothes from buckets	Bed making
Preparing meals	cleaning utility table	Lifting heavy buckets of wet clothes
Washing dishes	Ironing	Lifting young children
Dusting furniture and Floors		
Sweeping kitchen floor		

For proper utilization of energy, a few factors that are directly involved in energy management are discussed under body mechanic.

5.4   Efforts Used In Home Making Activities

Whatever may be the activity or the job to be performed, it requires several types of efforts like mental effort, visual effort, manual effort, tarsal effort and pedal effort. Each effort demands different quantity of energy expenditure.

Mental effort is required to do any task, even the routine tasks like cooking cleaning, washing, etc. though these tasks are performed daily, still one has to think about the way in which it has to be performed and mentally organise the task in sequence.

All the activities involve visual effort, although we are not aware of it. Muscular movement of the eye and adjustment of vision to the object at different distances and lighting conditions continuously take place while performing any work. This requires energy. Manual effort is required for all the household activities to be performed like cooking, cleaning, mapping, washing etc.

Torsal effort involves movement of the torsal and hence is termed as torsal efforts. These include bending, leaning, raising, turning etc. These are needed in doing more strenuous activities and demand higher energy costs.

Some of the activities in the house involve use of legs and feet movement i.e., standing, walking, climbing stairs etc. Since the whole body needs to be moved around these activities have heavy energy demands. It is called pedal efforts.

Houschold activities require a combination of more than one type of effort. In ordered to have well balanced energy expenditure pattern, the home maker needs to know the energy cost of various activities and also which activity is most tiring one. The energy costs are calculated based on oxygen consumption per minute or on heart rate (beats per minute).

5.5   Ways of Controlling Energy Expenditure

There are many ways which can control energy expenditure and reduce fatigue. But all methods do not suit to every situation. The person performing the activities and the type of activity are deciding factors in choosing the methods of controlling energy expenditure.

In any given job, energy consumption can be reduced by,

1) Developing an improved mental attitude towards the work to be done.
2) Eliminating unnecessary steps or combining new steps and processes in work
3) Arranging steps in any activities in a sequence
4) Using efficient equipment and other materials for convenience.
5) Arranging needed equipment and other materials according to convenience.
6) Maintaining correct body posture while working
7) Developing rhythm in doing work.
8) Improving skills and techniques.
9) Doing work with rightly spaced adequate rest periods.
10) Developing motivating conditions in work situations.
11) Body Mechanics

5.6   Body mechanics

Body mechanics deals with the body movement. It is defined as the "Science dealing with body forces and motions". The word 'mechanics' suggests a relationship to the functioning of the body. As was aptly stated by Esther Crew Bratton your own body constitutes your most important item of household equipment. It is well worth the effort it takes to acquire understanding of how the body functions in work and to develop skill in using the body effectively.

5.6.1 Principles of Body Mechanics

There are 5 important principles of body mechanics as given below.
1) Keeping the body parts in alignment.
2) Using muscles effectively.
3) Rhythm in movements.
4) Considering the center of gravity both of the body and of articles handled.
5) Taking advantage of momentum.

1) Keeping Body Parts in Alignment:

Keeping body parts in alignment results in stability when the various body weights are correctly positioned each centered over the base of support.

When any part of the body gets out of line, muscular effort is required to maintain body balance in addition to whatever work the body is doing, thus extra strain results. Therefore, correct or the right posture should be maintained by the person. For the correct posture whether sitting, standing or using a tool, muscles are so constructed specially to do certain things or does the job that no strain is felt by the person, while in incorrect posture, muscles which are not constructed for that particular job, do the job, and therefore strain and tension is felt by the worker. When the strain is felt, extra energy is spent. Hence for correct energy management, it is necessary to maintain the body parts aligned properly.

2) Using Muscles Effectively:

Using muscles effectively includes employing,

The strongest muscle feasible,

Setting the muscles that are to do the work before contacting the load,

Contracting muscles slowly, and Using muscles rhythmically.

For example, leg muscles, being-stronger than back muscles, should be used for lifting loads, This is accomplished by standing or kneeling close to the load and lifting with a slow, steady pull

Study of muscles used in performing work indicates that the smaller muscles become fatigued more quickly than the larger ones, though use of the smaller muscles involves the expenditure of less energy. Hence, in household processes, such as cutting and chopping, the arm muscles should be used instead of those of the hand and wrist.

One more point to be noted concerning muscles itself that, muscles exerts its greatest force when extended, and force diminishes as the muscle shortens. Hence, when lifting a heavy sofa, the legs should be slightly bent before grasping the load.

3) Rhythm in movement:

Rhythm in muscular performance may be defined as the repetition of movements at the same tempo. In the rhythmical activity, a large part of the first excitement still serves for the second, and the second for the third and so on. Inhibitions fall away, and the mere after effect of each stimulus secures a great saving for the new impulse. Thus it saves energy in regular rhythmic movements. Bratton explains why rhythmic work is less tiring than non-rhythmic, as based on the existence of double sets of muscles for accomplishing work. When they work rhythmically, one set rests while the other set works. In non-rhythmic work both sets may operate at the same time thereby making the work more tiring.

In the household many activities can be done rhythmically. For example, in dishwashing, when all the plates of one size are washed in sequence, the hands and arms develop certain rhythmic movements in handling them. Sweeping, running the vacuum cleaner and ironing clothes, all provide recognized possibilities for a regular flow of motions, resulting in rhythmic movements. In this manner, rhythmic motions help a great deal in managing energy effectively.

4) Considering Centre of Gravity of the Body:

Considering the centre of gravity is of importance in lifting, supporting, or carrying a load and also in reaching to get an object. It is always desirable to keep the load close to the body so that centre of gravity is taken care of.

Note in the above figure, how much closer the baby is to the women's body is good as pared to the poor method of lifting. The custom of carrying the baby on the mother's back, as the Japanese do, is an example of keeping the load close to the body, thereby walking along the centre of gravity.

Secondly, as far as possible, keeping the centre of the weight of the object through the centre of the body, and avoiding twisting the body helps in better energy management. Applying force to the centre of gravity of a load to be moved is the economical use of energy.

5) Taking Advantage of Momentum:

Taking advantage of momentum means the avoidance of stops and starts, and of change of speeds. Similar to rhythmic movements, free flowing motions are the least fatiguing of movements because they are continued so that one motion flows smoothly into the next, rather stopping abruptly. For instance, in polishing or dusting a large surface, the end of each movement may be rounded to make the next stroke a continuation of the forward stroke so that momentum of the work is maintained.

5.6.2 Posture

Body positions and motions are the key to effective body use. The feeling of comfort and discomfort are the results of the positioning of body weights, use of muscles and the use of skeletal system. Posture involves keeping the natural balance of the body stable, whether sitting, standing or moving.

According to Gross et.al (1973) "In correct posture, whether standing, sitting, or using a tool, muscles constructed to do certain things do them. In incorrect posture, muscles not so constructed must do the job". When any part of the body gets out of line, muscular effort is required to maintain body in balance in addition to what ever work the body is doing.

To avoid strain and to develop a good body carriage while working, some attention should be given to posture habits in standing, sitting, stooping and bending while at work. Good posture in doing any task may define as the position which requires the expenditure of the smallest amount of energy.

A good standing posture is one in which the head, neck, chest and abdomen are balanced vertically one upon the other, so 'that the weight is carried mainly by the bony framework and a minimum of effort and strain is placed upon the muscles and ligaments. When the body is well balanced in the standing position, the head will be directly over the feet, and the center of gravity will pass through the middle of the face, nose, shoulder, hip, the outside of the knee, and the outside of the ankle.

A good sitting posture for work is well- balanced and poised position. The weight is carried by the bony support of the skeleton thus relieving the muscles and nerves of all strain. The poise is such that minimum adjustment is necessary for such action as the work may demand. The line of gravity falls through the middle of the shoulders, hips and seat bones. The body is straight from hips to neck, and there is no flex or bend at the waistline.

Poor standing and sitting postures may result in permanent changes in the spine in positions of the joints, ligaments and muscles and in the location of the organs of the body. Such changes produce strain and tensions which increase the fatigue costs of homemaking tasks.

Using the most comfortable body position while working eases the body and relieves the strain. Alternating standing and sitting is more restful than either one continued for a long period.

In bending to do certain tasks, it is easier to put one foot slightly forward and bend through the knee and ankle joint. In lifting something heavy from the floor, such as a body or a bag of groceries, it is better to bend the knees and thigh joints and use the stronger leg muscles for the actual lifting. Pushing or pulling a large piece of furniture can be done with least strain by dropping into a partial crouch, knees limber, hips low, and pulling or pushing in that position. Carrying packages or other articles is easier when the load can rest against the hip. Balancing is done by bending toward the other side which shifts the weight to the large bones and leg muscles. That is why we find most of the labourers carrying their load at their backs and resting them on their hips.

5.6.3 Body Forces

Pushing, pulling and lifting are the three important activities in which the body forces are applied. All five principles of body mechanics have to be taken into consideration while performing these activities.

To push near the top of the back of a heavy chair to move it is more effective for tipping it over than for moving it along the floor. If the force of the push is to be effective it must be applied at the level of the center of gravity of the object and in the direction the object is to move. To do this one should crouch before the effort and then apply the force for the push while coming out of the crouch. This will insure that the major part of the force will come from the large and strong muscles of the thighs and legs as they come out of the large crouch. This will relieve and protect from injury of the smaller and weaker muscles of the back.

The person exerts the required force with the least possible muscular effort. Forces exerted by the hands and forearm originates from a right-angled bend at the elbow. Force exerted downward from the elbow joint rather than upwards or sidewise. For moving heavy weights, force exerted at or near the center of gravity of the weight. For lifting heavy weights, force is exerted as near as possible to the center of gravity of the worker's body. Force exerted from a stable position of the worker's body. Force for moving heavy objects exerted by the large, strong muscles of the legs and thighs when straightening out from a crouch rather than by the muscles of a straightened arm or the small muscles of the back.

5.6.4 Fatigue Forms and Causes

Introduction

Fatigue means tiredness from physical work or lowered capacity to perform subsequent work. On the basis of anatomy of the body, if after work, body's capacity to do the work reduces or the body is unable to do the work as before, it is called fatigue. Inability to do the work is either due to over-work i.e more than one's capacity or doing those jobs in which the individual is not interested.

Circumstances such as deadlines, emotional stress, insufficient information, or knowledge and information overload contribute to fatigue and stress. Mental overload may cause the physiological changes like increase in heart rate, increased respiration, elevated blood pressure etc.

Fatigue is not easily defined. It manifests itself in different forms and yet they are the closely related forms. In simple words, the feeling of tiredness and the desire to stop working after doing some amount of work is called fatigue. Thus when fatigued, our body's capacity to do work is reduced. Fatigue signifies a reduced performance of work. It is caused by physical exhaustion, aversion to work, preoccupation with some other aspects of life or any combination of these and other factors.

5.6.5 Forms of Fatigue

Fatigue can either be psychological or physiological. Due to fatigue, our body's capacity to do work is reduced. In order to avoid fatigue, either rest period should be introduced between the work or the job should be made more interesting. Besides these, the workercan either be appreciated or given some incentive, so that the worker gets motivated to do work more efficiently and effectively. There are basically two types of fatigue. They are:

The physiological fatigue: Sometimes also called tissue physical impairment.

The non-physiological or psychological fatigue or subjective fatigue: This psychological fatigue can again be subdivided into two types i.e. boredom and frustration.

Physiological Fatigue:

It is the fatigue occurred due to the physical exhaustion. A study of the fatigue of homemakers with young children illustrates some of the problems in managing home related work. The number of tasks within a given period of time and shifting from task to task were factors closely related to the fatigue these homemakers experienced. Attitudes toward household tasks and the energy demands of specific tasks, combined with personal feelings of adequacy in carrying out the activities, and the characteristics of the work place have been related to feelings of fatigue.

Haqqard and Greenberg define it as incapacity for exertion induced by previous exertion. This capacity is restored only by rest. After taking rest the lost energy can be regained and we can continue to work further. During the muscular activity, the body consumes fuel and gives out energy. The energy producing material in the muscle is mainly glycogen, which is formed by muscle tissue from sugar products brought to it by the blood. In muscular work, glycogen unites with oxygen in the blood stream, releases energy and forms lactic acid and carbon-di-Oxide (CO_2), Both these waste products interfere with continued muscular activity of the body.

This state of the body results in a feeling of tiredness which is termed as physiological fatigue. The process of accumulation of lactic acid and CO_2 can be represented as:

Glucose + O_2 = Energy + Lactic Acid + CO_2

Recovery or the removal of lactic acid and CO_2 in the muscles is necessary after any and every kind of work. The blood stream picks up' CO_2 and carries it to the lungs where it is exhaled. At the same time, the blood brings Oxygen to the muscles, and lactic acid is oxidized and reconverted to glycogen. Thus oxygen helps to prevent fatigue by aiding removal of lactic acid in the muscles. However, this can be done only if the body is at rest, and does not release any more lactic acid. If the body continues to work, the oxygen supplied will be used up by glycogen for the release of energy, making the oxygen unavailable for the removal of lactic acid from the muscles. That is why a person gets totally exhausted while doing continuous work.

Posture and use of the body muscles are also very important in performing a task. Imbalanced posture while performing a task and inefficient use of these muscles and muscular effort causes physiological fatigue keeping the body parts and major body weights in well aligned position is essential to avoid fatigue at work.

Psychological Fatigue:

Sometimes fatigue may occur even when there is enough energy to do work. This will also result in reduced output. This is called as psychological fatigue. Just as physiological fatigue results in a reduced output of work and aversion to work, similarly, psychological fatigue too results in an aversion to work further and reduced output. It is very difficult to define or measure, as it consists in rather vague subjective states. It is not localized in the body. This can be classified into two types- Frustration fatigue which looks to the individual himself and boredom fatigue which looks to the environment as the basis of fatigue.

This is further divided into two types:

1. Boredom Fatigue

2. Frustration Fatigue

1. Boredom Fatigue:

This results from the non-coincidence of experiencing two durations of time, that of work being slow and irksome, and that of the mind which longs to be else where. We experience the activity as continuing without change where as the mind is ready and eager for change. Studies have shown that the bored , time at work was judged longer than to those not bored. Those workers who were most frequently bored made the greatest number of complaints concerning working conditions. It appears probable that boredom increases sensitivity to objectionable features connected with work; such as noise, atmospheric conditions, troublesome materials, etc. Nelson and Bartley found the most boring period to be last hour of both morning and afternoon work periods. In boredom fatigue time seems to pass very slowly.

2. Frustration Fatigue:

Besides boredom fatigue another type of psychological fatigue is the frustration fatigue. This may be regarded as an experimental pattern arising in a conflict situation in which the general alignment of the individual may be described as an aversion. This particular pattern involves feelings of limpness, bodily discomfort, and general tension which are undesirable as well as result in inadequacy for activity.

These feelings of discomfort and aversion to work should not be considered as symptoms of fatigue but they are the fatigue itself.

When plans fail to work out and goals cannot be reached or when conflict situations arise which call for the weighing of alternatives in the making of decisions, and the seeking of new goals, a person may experience feelings of frustration and increased tensions. Fatigue which results from such conflicts is a part of the total picture of frustration. Therefore, this kind of a fatigue is termed as frustration fatigue.

5.6.6 Causes of Fatigue

As a background for considering the physiological and psychological aspects of fatigue, we can look at some common situations in which we experience fatigue, situations that are often associated with feelings of tiredness. These situations can be summarized in a nontechnical way:

1) A long period of mental or light physical work in a restricted or uncomfortable position.
2) A long period of work in a standing position.
3) A long period of making continuous postural adjustments, such as when riding in a car.
4) A period, possibly short, of heavy physical exertion.
5) Working at a disliked task.
6) Working at an unaccustomed task.
7) Working at a task that requires close attention or extreme alertness.
8) Working under pressure, for instance, when meeting a deadline.
9) Working without sufficient knowledge or information.
10) Emotional stress, whether working or not.

Nickel et,al.(1976) described the causes of fatigue in three domains:

Worker domain:

The physical energy required for the performance of the task. The pace of work, the tools used and the position of the worker are among the factors affecting energy use in the household work.

Incorrect posture and inefficient use of efforts while performing the work will cause fatigue. Hazelton and Russell describe efficient use as the one that 1) uses only those muscles or parts of the body that are necessary to the operatio, and 2) uses those muscles or parts of the body that are best able to do the work. In lifting a heavy baby or a bag of groceries from the floor, stronger leg muscles can be utilized if a person bends the knees and hips. If the worker needs only at the hips, he or she is using weaker back muscles and is ignoring this principle of efficiency in body mechanics.

There are related principles that apply to weight and body movement. Lifted objects carried close to the middle of the body require less effort than if they are carried away from the body. Smooth, continues and rhythmic motions are less tiring than sudden, sharp changes in movement.

Domain: The Nature of Work

Home related work is varied, demanding, and requires specific current knowledge. Teacher, chef, counselor, chauffeur, gardener, interior decorator, and purchasing agent are some of the more specific occupational roles combined in the role of home maker. Also, full time homemakers manage other role, such as that of husband, wife, mother, father, or neighbor, along with the specific corresponding demands.

If the work process is not properly analysed, timed and performed in the right method it adds to the fatigue of the home maker.

The Work Environment

Inappropriate work climate, work areas, work station heights/depths and work centre cause fatigue to the worker. The work centre includes equipment, supplies, storages space and work surface. Any one incorrect aspect will lead to fatigue.

Bartley indicates a number of typically fatigue- producing situations including paced performance; prolonged activity; action in the face of remoteness of goals; frustrating situations; inadequacy; and interaction with the environment- too exacting for a specific body mechanism.

The complexity of fatigue concepts is emphasized by Ryan and Smith (1954:287):

"The term fatigue has been used in many different senses and in fact it is not a term referring to a single unitary phenomenon. Instead it is a blanket term for many different effects of work-all of those effects which are harmful or deleterious, and which are a function of the duration and amount of effort, but which are recoverable through rest. Thus pnly the beneficial effects of exercise and learning, and the drastic effects resulting in permanent damage are excluded from the concept."

Ryan and Smith suggest four different kinds of effects of work which have been termed"fatigue":

1. Feeling of weariness tiredness, exhaustion, unwillingness to continue work, aches and pains attributed to work.

2. Deterioration in ability to perform the work itself.(Loss of capacity for the work.)

3. Deterioration in ability to perform other tasks and activities (Transfer of fatigue.)

4. A large number of physiological changes-in blood chemistry and structure, excretory products, glandular secretions, etc."

Knowles found some evidence of frustration fatigue in her discussions with homemakers regarding their attitudes toward certain tasks. Some of the reasons given for disliking tasks were:

1) Uncertainty and confusion in performance
2) Conflicting standards within the family group and inability to satisfy all members.
3) Unfavorable working conditions.
4) Practices and standards of work conditioned by tradition and in conflict with new developments and methods, and,
5) Time required by the task could be used for other more interesting activities.

Thus, we find that there are a number of reasons for frustration fatigue. However, they can be broadly put under three categories. **In the first** instance, frustration fatigue may arise from the job itself. For example, the inexperienced person whose first pie or first slip cover is something short of success and which might take longer to be completed may feel utterly fatigued.

The long period of work may be the result of interruptions and clutter and so the worker will complain of the feeling of fatigue.

Secondly, fatigue may arise from competition between what one is doing and what one would like to do. The homemaker working at home may feel fatigued when she know that kitty party is in full swing next door which she wants to attend but due to loads of work at home she cannot, so she will complain of fatigue and try to avoid doing the work at home.

Finally, fatigue may arise from something entirely unrelated to whatever one is doing. For example, the homemaker working at home may feel fatigued as she knows her child has not arrived back from the school or a serious illness in the family may make her simple household jobs very fatiguing.

Bartley indicates a number of typically fatigue-producing situations including paced performance; prolonged activity; action in the face of remoteness of goals; frustrating situations; inadequacy; and interaction with the environment-too exacting for a specific body mechanism.

5.6.7 Methods of Relieving Fatigue

The home maker can take some of the steps listed below to remove or avoid fatigue, so that she can continue to perform her works.

1. Rest Periods

The first method of removing fatigue is introducing rest periods in between the work. Rest periods are of value both for increasing output and for alleviating fatigue. The kind or rest periods should be related to the kind of fatigue, to be most effective. The effectiveness of a rest period is related to the completeness of relaxation.

To alleviate physiological fatigue, there must be cessation of physical activity to allow time for fatigue products to be removed from the body and in the cases of greater fatigue, time for the store of glycogen to be replenished. Only in sleep the body can entirely eliminate physiological fatigue.

2. Change of Tasks

There is frequent confusion between local muscle discomfort and fatigue. Change of task will lessen this discomfort. If a housewife is required to perform an exceedingly painstaking task for only a part of the day and is shifted to work which requires much less concentration and the use of different muscles, the output is found to improve. The homemaker is responsible for a variety of tasks and may easily alternate types of work. Since energy expenditure is still occurring at a normal rate, this type of rest period cannot be expected to eliminate much physical fatigue but is satisfactory for both boredom and frustration fatigue.

3. Putting Interest into the Job

In reducing boredom fatigue, it is wise to remember that small changes in the task may be helpful, or that interest outside the job may be introduced, such as listening to music. Mayo suggests that a job may be made more interesting by the simple device of setting intermediate goals which are easily attainable, thus avoiding the seemingly endlessness of the job ahead. For instance, the woman who tries to complete the stacking and then sets another goal feels a glow of accomplishment and a stimulus to speed more quickly than the person who hopes to complete the dishwashing in thirty minutes, but does not know until the end whether or not she has succeeded. Another suggestion for making tasks more interesting is to work in groups. While one of the characteristics of the homemaker's work is her isolation, there are possibilities for making the home tasks made more interesting if some of the jobs can be organized as a group rather than as individual ones. Laundering can be more pleasant if one person carries the clothes to the line while another person prepares a fresh tubful for hanging.

4. An Analytical Approach to a Job

This comes through changed procedure and actually reduces the physiological fatigue and at the same time creates interest in the work itself. For instance, a young girl will take more interest if she has to prepare the entire dinner including the entire dessert course than if she is asked to mash the~ potatoes, slice the bread, pour the water and do numerous other routine jobs. Besides these, there are more ways to remove the feeling of fatigue and better energy management.

5. Having Proper Work Place and Proper Equipment

Such as good environmental conditions, proper equipment like the table according to the homemaker's height, adjustable shelves in the kitchen, etc. can also aid in reducing fatigue.

6. Appreciation of the Work

When the home maker is appreciated by the family members for her work, it motivates her to do the work more effectively, without any complaints of feeling fatigued and appreciation also as an incentive for the worker.

7. Giving Incentive to the Worker

The homemaker can give incentive to her children to do work, like promise them that she will take them out if they help her in the work. Similarly, the worker herself can find incentives for herself, like an ice-cream, an outing to meet friends, etc. while deciding to take up and finish the work with in the specified period.

Swanson S.B (1981) has given some methods to reduce the different types of fatigue occurring due to particular work or activity.

Fatigue caused by boredom can be reduced by frequent work interruptions. It can also be reduced by altering the physical environment.

Frustration fatigue can be reduced by isolating the causal factor and dealing with it.

Use of work simplification methods can alleviate fatigue.

5.6.8 Stress and Its Management

Stress may be defined in its medical sense as "essentially the rate of the wear and tear caused by life". The rate of wear and tear stems from both physical and emotional causes. We are now becoming aware of the part of physical environment in causing stress. "Stress and psychosomatic diseases stem in part from environmental factors which the ecologist senses but cannot state in medical terms. Stress is vaguely understood when one feels that what is doing is strenuous or wearing. He has subjective sensations of just being tired", feeling jittery or generally ill.

Stress and fatigue have something in common in patterns of inducement and chain of consequences that tend to disrupt the balanced routine of the body. Selye describes the conditions of stress at the biochemical and physical level. He found adrenal stimulation, shrinkage of lymphatic organs, intestinal disturbance and other bodily changes as constituting stress.

Stress occurs when the individual completing task assignment feels pressured, functions in an inadequate environmental situation, lacks sufficient or operable materials and equipment, or has damaging communication with supervisors.

Healthy Tips for Stress-related Fatigue Management:

1) Adopt a positive mental approach to exercises and diet, and try to make them a part of your daily routine.
2) Adopt a healthy life style by incorporating Yoga and Meditation in your routine.
3) Involve yourself in recreational activities such as reading, watching T.V. listening to music etc.
4) As far as possible try to walk the distance to your home, office, shopping area, instead of traveling by a vehicle.
5) Involve yourself in hobbies such as embroidery, sewing, gardening etc.
6) Involve in outdoor games such as swimming, tennis, badminton, cricket etc. This can be made to have more fun if the entire family takes part together in these games.
7) Avoid eating fat-rich foods as stress-busters. Instead, change the kind of work you are involved in. Take a break like reading, taking a walk, listening to music, talking to a friend or a relative in between strenuous physical work.
8) Change the mind-set of the family members by distributing housework among them and ease your workload.
9) Group activities in the household should be encouraged by involving children and husband in household work.
10) Avoid as far as possible arguments in the house and office affairs. Try to understand that just as you have an opinion, others too have a right to voice their opinion. Talk softly and try to reach a compromise.

Following these tips would not only reduce stress-related or bodily-related fatigue, but will also make family living enjoyable and comfortable. These guidelines would provide a long lasting, satisfying and healthy atmosphere for the stress-enriched fast-moving lives in the modern homes.

5.7   Energy management In Home Related Activities
Introduction
Human energy required for the performance of any task is a combination of normal body functions respiration circulation, secretion and excretion-and the energy used to move about and to complete the task. The pace of work, the tools

used, and the positions of the worker are among the factors affecting energy use in household work.

Managing Home Related Activities

Measuring the energy costs of household tasks, though useful in planning work and in designing living units, provides only a partial understanding of the fatigue the worker experiences. Some light tasks, listed in table 43.1, may be tiring because of personal attitudes, postural strain, muscle tension, or the concentration and skill required. Other energy-demanding tasks may be less tiring than light work because of the cognitive or affective resources of the worker.

The natural capacity of the muscles to produce energy without fatigue is another factor that needs to be understood when evaluating the significance of energy-cost studies for the work in home. Of the total rate of energy expenditure which represents the capacity of the body to work without accumulating fatigue products in muscles, Passmore and Durnin (1955:833) Say: "... in order to prevent evidence of fatigue the intensity of the working rate and the length of the compensating rest pauses must be so adjusted as to give gross over-all rates of energy expenditure of not more than 5 Cal/min.

5.7.1 Approximate energy costs for selected activities

Work Calories per minute	Activities	
No work 1 Cal/min	Resting	
Light 1-2 Cal/min	Sedentary activities Sewing Knitting Paring potatoes Machine sewing Operating a vacuum sweeper.	Standing activities Ironing Beating with rotary beater Dishwashing Reaching to 22 inches above floor Reaching to 72 inches above floor

Moderate 2-3 Cal/min	Walking Sweeping Dust mopping Appling floor wax, long-handled applicator Hanging clothes from basket on floor or table Playing piano
Heavy 3-4 Cal/min	Washing floor Waxing floor Bed making to three inches above the floor Cleaning carpeted stairs
Very heavy Over 4 Cal/min	Going downstairs, from floor Dancing Gardening, Weeding

The meaning here is that when there is a steady expenditure of energy of 5 Calories or more per minute in a working day, the circulatory system could not continuously carry away from the muscles the waste products of oxidation. At this rate of energy expenditure, moreover, the heat produced from oxidation in muscles would not be dissipated rapidly enough and the body temperature would rise. Both of these effects would result in decreasing the capacity to continue work.

Appropriate energy management is related to three important components of the task performance

5.7.2 The Worker

The worker is the person performing the job or the task. The cost of worker input will have four broad components.

- The affective component. Attitudes, feelings, and interests.
- The cognitive component. Knowledge, thought processes, and skills.
- The temporal component. The time of the worker and the timing of tasks.
- The physical component. The use of the body in the work

The Affective Component

Affective component is concerned with the worker's personal feelings about the activity –his attitude and interests, his preferences and dislikes. These aspects may contribute to the homemaker's feelings of working hard and easily. Feelings of working easily may contribute to greater satisfaction with the work.

Feelings of working hard may be directly related to the unhappy feeling that we are doing more than necessary to accomplish the work.

It is more difficult to do those activities that we dislike compared to those we like – it takes more out of us emotionally for we do not enjoy the time spent and it ids not satisfying.

Dissatisfaction with work may have many deleterious consequences. Feelings of tiredness and fatigue may become chronic. The accomplishment of work-oriented goals may be hampered. The dissatisfaction may permeate other aspects of our lives and into the lives of others.

Work has an influence on many sides of our life. If we are unhappy in our work, this unhappiness has its effect on our home life. If we are happy with what we do and the people with whom we work, then this satisfaction contributes to more satisfying and other richer living outside the work situation.

The Cognitive Component

The cognitive component describes the contribution of thinking –using knowledge, setting and defining goals, makinf plans, paying attention during work, making many judgments as the work progresses so that the activity can be controlled, and developing and using habits and skills.

As the homemaker performs the work of the home, she uses knowledge based on formal and informal study and on experience, she makes plans, judgments, decisions and assumes responsibility for them. She pays attention to the task or tasks, mentally processing information as the work progresses partly a mental attribute. All of this constitutes the intellectual dimensions of the workers input, one of the determinants in ease of work and in job satisfaction.

The cognitive component serves two functions. One is to plan and coordinate the use of resources prior to action. Resources external to the homemaker, such as money, material goods, supplies and the personal contributions of other family members are considered. The other personal contributions of the homemaker are also coordinated with her intellectual contribution.

The second broad function of the cognitive component is to bridge the gap between the goal or stated task and its accomplishment . Mental activities are needed to carry out or perform the activity and produce results.

In performing these two broad functions, the homemaker might be thought of as a system that handles information, various inputs are required to determine the use of resources, interrelated elements exists within the system to produce output, the output is the resources use of the family. The cognitive component is concerned with processes involved within the system for receiving and using the information, i.e for handling the information. It is through understanding the processes involved in handling information that the management specialist can help achieve an organized approach to solving problems in work and workplace design.

The Temporal Component

The time contributed by the homemaker in doing the work of the home is part of her nonphysical input. So is her time for employment work. The time contribution includes not only the total amount of time for action but the timing of the events. Too often the total amount of time and the allocation among homemaking tasks is considered the total contribution.

Time provides an organizing medium for our lives, a common denominator within which we operate. Time does not change with the events that take place within it. Time represents a succession of events and therefore change happens. Appreciation of some of the consequences of living in time provides a frame of reference.

An objective of studying the temporal component of the cost of work is to identify those underlying operations that will permit us to gain the most satisfaction from use of time.

Control of time requires recognition of the interrelatedness of the past, present and the future. The past, present and future are represented in the succession of events. The present is always changing to become part of the past. The passage of time shows the constant change that is taking place.

One of the costs of the temporal component is the integration that we must make of the past and present and the anticipation of the future.

The proportion of allocation of time may vary from time to time and person to person. A homemaker may have certain freedom in timing her activities. But the important constraint is inflexible events, the nature of household work and the home maker preferences. It is important to realize that, with time, we can structure our lives so that we are carrying out those activities that are the more satisfying to us.

The physical component

The physical component deals with the skeletal structure, the muscle action and the circulation system of the human body or the worker and the physical work environment.

The physical cost s of the work of the home are tobe thought of in terms of effects on all the systems of the body that function during work. Energy expenditure is relatively light for many of the jobs in today's homes and is unlikely to be correlated with fatigue. The maintenance of working position is sometimes the most fatiguing aspect of the job. Movements made during work performance may constitute beneficial exercise or they can subject parts of the body to stresses that are fatiguing or detrimental to general well-being.

The worker body constitutes her most important item of household equipment.

The physical cost of work is the study of energy expenditure to each task. The amount of energy used is studied in two ways, i.e Direct method and indirect method.

First by the measurement of heat given off by the body (as a result of oxidation within the body), and second, by the measurement of both oxygen used and carbon dioxide produced or by measuring only the amount of oxygen used. The first method , measuring the amount of heat produced is called direct calorimeter and requires the use of extremely delicate instruments inside an expensive heat-proof chamber. The other method , indirect calorimetry, requires less expensive equipment and simpler laboratories.

Either direct or indirect calorimeter is a means of measuring a rate of oxidation in the body as a whole. Because energy expenditure represents a rate of oxidation which occurs as muscles are used, energy cannot be saved and accumulated to produce a large store to be drawn upon at a time of greater need.

In order to develop an understanding of energy expenditure as a measure of the physical cost of work, it is more important to have a general knowledge of probable levels of energy expenditure for different kinds of activities than to know the specific average values resulting from any one study. There is a wide variation in results for even a standardized task from one subject to another and for any one subject from trial to trial.

Anyone of these components may assume unusual importance to one family and be relatively unimportant to another or to a given family at one stage and not at another. The affective component concerns the part that personal interests and attitudes play in making the work easy or difficult. The woman who likes to be "on the move" will not find a work method easier if it eliminates walking and requires her to remain for long in one spot. The cognitive component is the component of thinking. The knowledge the worker has of how to do the work and of the result desired, and the skill she has to produce the result, contribute importantly to ease of work. Time is generally considered an aspect of the homemaker's work and regarded as one of the resources with which the family's goals are achieved. Units of time provide an easily understood measure of the cost of work. The physical component of work is widely recognized. It is related to the energy expenditure for different activities.

5.7.3 The Work and the Work Place

A job may comprise a few or many responsibilities and activities or tasks. For the homemaker, the sum of her responsibilities is her job; the job comprises many tasks, such as dishwashing, meal preparation, bathing children, marketing, or shopping. Tasks, course, can be further divided into smaller units, and psychologically each unit may constitute a task. Grocery shopping may logically be the task as well as selecting the meat, fresh vegetables, or other items. The size of the task is variable.

The job or the work has to be described analysed, and evaluated. A job description provides the basis for job analysis and job evaluation. Ryan and Smith (1954:35) point out that description for selection an placement should include "what the worker does and how often, how his work is initiated, the degree and closeness of the supervision he receives, the extent to which his work is checked by others, the nature and consequences of errors, the place of the job in the organizational structure of the company, and numerous other observations, ratings, and data. . . ."

A job analysis of household work by Smith (1962) provides an example of another purpose that of providing a basis for house arrangement. Smith obtained a description of the person or persons performing the activity in the home, the time and location involved, the equipment and furnishings used, the frequency with which the activity was performed and the specific components of the activity.

Comprehensive analyses of homemaking work permit us to identify common requirements among the tasks as well as the variables. Job evaluation determines the relative order of importance of a series of jobs, based on the duties, responsibilities, and requirements for performance, by analysis, description, and evaluation of those factors in an orderly and systematic way."

The occupation of homemaking entails a variety of tasks, duties, and responsibilities. Most homemakers are both managers and workers. They are responsible for both mental and physical activity. They plan and carry out the plans, facilitating and evaluating them as action progresses. In many respects, the homemaker's managerial situation is similar to that of small farms and other small businesses. The variable work conditions, materials, and standards for the outcome contribute to the amount of mental work.

The goal of accomplishing household work is primarily a means to other ends, one of which is the development and socialization of the children. Work in homes is a child's first acquaintance with work-how satisfying or dissatisfying it is, how difficult or easy, how essential to his existence, how important to accept responsibility and to control and time events. Homemaking work can be vehicle for his experimentation with task accomplishment. Failure may be less costly when they occur within the shelter of the individuals own family.

Effective work methods, well learned, become standing rules that can be used to advantage to decrease attention during task planning and performance; standing rules also decrease the amount of planning that is needed. A routine sequence of steps, set in motion after a quick check for appropriateness to the present situation, permits a smooth flow of work that only a skilled person can achieve.

5.7.4 Purpose of studying work

The first purpose of studying work is to identify the demands made on the person. Household tasks are necessarily part of the problem of studying the use of the human resources in accomplishing work, for tasks are an output- the result of using the human resource in conjunction with other resources. The nature of the action is one determinant of the various human costs.

The second purpose is to identify the requirements needed in the workplace for the task and the person. Identification pf such requirements is a prerequisite to functional design. Such knowledge will permit the manufacture, builder and the work specialist to build into the design of equipment and workplaces those characteristics that will automatically minimize worker input. Equipment and work places, as well as the work , are part of the problem of studying the use of the human resource for work since they help or hinder the implementation of the action.

The third purpose is to obtain the background to guide the functional placement and arrangement of workplaces. The placement of the objects used in work as well as their design and quality, determined the human costs of using them. Knowledge of work provides an important basis for determining guides for placement and arrangement of workplaces.

5.8   Management of Energy Applied To Workplace Design
Introduction

Workplaces are a major part of the team that is needed to accomplish household tasks. The quality of the design of the workplace in terms of requirements of the task and of the worker has an important effect on the ease with which the action is accomplished. The problem of relating task and worker requirements for design of workplace is described by the term functional design.

5.8.1 Functional Design of the Workplace

The functional design is the arrangement of the important parts to serve a special purpose. Applied to household workplaces, we say that a functional design for a workplace is a design meeting the requirements of the work and the worker. Our problem is to determine and coordinate the requirements of the task and worker.

Functional design should result in minimum of strain on the worker and require a minimum of effort to do the activity. Availability of needed space, items, and facilities makes it possible for the worker to dothe work without allocating much attention to the situation itself. One set of conditions is not satisfactory for all household tasks. Many tasks require a particular setup due to requirements for specialized equipment or facilities, type of supplies, and work surface on which to manipulate items or carry out processes. Characteristics of each part of the workplace must be designed to facilitate the performance of the specific task.

The equipment, storage, and work-surface requirements for a work place are determined primarily by the nature of the activity, but these must be tempered by the worker's requirements if the design is to truly functional.

To develop the physical design of workplaces, a number of aspects must be considered:

- Location in vertical space
- Height of work surfaces
  Height of shelves, drawers, bins
  Height of appliances or their parts
  Weight and size of items to be stored
- Location in horizontal space
- Supplies, tools
  Adjacent workplaces-height
- Spatial arrangement of parts
- Work surface-appliance relationship
  Distribution of work surface
  Location of drawers, doors, bins
  Location of controls
- Amount and dimensions and space for Work (length and width of surface; depth of basins)

- Worker at work-one and more than one
- Storage of supplies and other items
- Provision of special features
- Utilities (electricity, gas, water; drainage)
- Duplication of facilities
- Ventilation
- Lighting

Task and worker requirements must be related to each of these aspects to achieve a functional design. Some of the good work surface and equipment design are shown in the following pictures as given by Nickel et.al (1942)

5.8.2 Work Surface

The dimensions for the three parts of work surfaces must be planned separately: the height, width, and depth. The total amount of surface needed for the task and the allocation of the surface are related considerations.

The height of the work surface must be keyed to the worker requirement of maintaining good working posture. The width of the surface (side-to-side measure) is probably more closely related to task needs than to worker needs if a minimum 18 inches for standing space is provided. The functional limits for the width of work areas range from 48 to 58 inches for the maximum and 40 inches for the normal work area.

The depth of the surface (front-to-back measure) is determined by three factors: the distance that can be reached comfortably, the activity, and the items that must be used and stored temporarily during use. The normal working-area depth of 14 to 16 inches for women and the maximum work-area depth of 24 inches suggest that much of the activity that involves manipulative motions may be done within the 14 to 16 inch range, but the 24-inch distance is not an excessive depth for the work surface since it can be reached without assuming an off balance position.

Storage

5.8.3 Three principles provide the basic directives for functional storage.
Principle 1.
Store Frequently Used Items at Place of First Use

Those things that are used more often should be given priority since their availability will have a greater effect on the amount of work. Storage at place of first use generally has merits over storage at place of last use.

Principle 2.
Place items so:

They are easy to see, reach, grasp, and replace. This principle favors reduction of mental and physical effort, time, and dissatisfaction. Visibility and accessibility are the key factors. Feelings of better organization and greater ease of work were expressed with more functional storage.

Principle 3.

- **Determine the Worker's Limits of Reach.**

  This principle is specifically directed toward keying the physical limitations of the main worker, with respect to her reach, (below figure) to the design of the storage and placement of items within it. The maximum reach upward helps to determine the height of the top shelf; the level must permit the worker to grasp items from the shelf, but, if the worker reaches across a surface to the shelf, the reaching height is reduced. For these reasons, the distance must be carefully determined.

- **Principles of Storage:**

  Certain principles of storage of equipment and tools if followed will help to improve work arrangement at various work centers as given below (Varghese et.al)

- **Storage of tools and supplies at the place of first use,**

  e.g. knives, spoons, sieves, chopper, etc. should be kept at the preparation center. Utensil used in cooking, spices, supplies such as flour, rice, etc, should be stored near cooking center. Laundry supplies should be in the bath room or the place where clothes are washed.

- **Duplication of inexpensive materials and equipment needed in more than one place:**

  For instance, two separate brooms should be kept, one for the kitchen floor and another for other rooms. Dish towels at sink center and also hand towels at cooking center. Laddles and serving spoons at the preparation center and also in the serving center or dining area. Such duplication minimizes walking motions, search for things when needed.

Placing of all materials and equipment used in a single type of process in general area in which the process is to be carried on, e.g. cups, plates, water tumblers should be stored closer to dining area. Bed linen for all bed rooms in a central place.

Storage of items, so that they are easy to see, easy to reach, and easy to grasp, e.g. pots and pans when stacked together need extra searching motions, hence these can be arranged by storing small ones in front of the large ones in a single row for clear visibility. Plates may be arranged in vertical slots on a rack. Tea spoons, table spoons, serving spoons each type should be sorted out and stored in divided drawer or in cloth bags.

- **Guidelines for Better Storage:**

Sort Items to Be Stored According to the Function of the Center.

2. Store unlike Items One Row Deep and One Layer Deep.

3. Stack Only Those Items Having the Same Dimensions.

4. Provide Sufficient Clearance for Grasping and Replacing Items.

5. Place Frequently Used, Heavy Items within Normal Reach.

6. Organize Items within the Storage Space to Reduce the Search and Facilitate the Flow of Motions.

- **Appliances:**

The design of the appliance, a third part of many centers, should be analyzed to determine the effect on the content of the work as well as the effect on the worker's input. Identify ways in which the design of the appliance affects the content of the job with respect to the type of action. The type and amount of physical action is also affected by the appliance design. The design of controls and their placement also play an important part in the amount of attention needed to use them. A careful analysis will be needed to determine how well the worker's abilities and limitations have been taken into account. The coordination of appliance design and the worker's physical inputs is a vital key to functional design of appliances. Directives already presented for work surface and storage design are appropriately applied to equivalents of using work levels and storage facilities in appliances

- **Space Allowances for Working:**

How much space should be allowed for the person to permit satisfactory performance of various activities? This and the related questions of space allowances for more than one worker and for passageways are relevant to the concept of functional arrangement of centers and workplaces. Cramped positions contribute to dissatisfaction with the working situation, dislike of the activity, and less effective performance of the task. Inadequate space for another person to walk past a worker or a workplace, through a hallway, or for one to go up and down stairs with a load requires restricted movement and extra attention to one's movement and positions

Three questions must be answered if adequate space is allowed for working: What is the basic position? What is the basic movement or elemental activity? Is additional space needed for part of an appliance or storage facility? The worker's basic position may be to stand, sit, walk, bend, squat, or kneel. The elemental activity may be to reach, carry, push; open doors, drawers; operate appliance; manipulate equipment, tools; arrange various items such as sheets, towels, supplies. A part of an appliance, storage facility, or furniture, such as a door or drawer, requires a certain amount of space when opened; space for this structural facility must be provided in addition to space for the person's basic position and activity.

5.9   Management Process Applied To Energy Expenditure
Introduction
Time and energy are two important human resources available to us, which must be used properly and not wasted. Homemakers have lot of responsibilities within the home and outside home; hence they must carefully study how they can improve their methods of work. Work simplification is the means of work improvement. Work simplification is achieved through application of scientific management. It is defined as "conscious seeking of the simplest, easiest and quickest method of doing work".

Planning Energy Use:
Since energy management is directly involved with the performance of work, the major decision in planning this resource is to solve the problems on when and how to perform the work. It would also require the careful decisions related not only to minimize energy expenditure, but also to avoid bodily discomfort and fatigue.

The problem on deciding when to do the work is interwoven with time planning. This involves the preparation of a time schedule in which light and heavy tasks are organized alternately. Besides this, there is a need to incorporate rest periods in between these two tasks. However, one should keep in mind hat certain tasks are fixed for certain time slots, as in the case of attending to school or work place, meal times, sleeping periods etc. Considering all these and taking into account one's availability and work demands, an individual should plan her energy use carefully.

Time and energy planning are inseparable. Managing energy is similar to managing time. It involves the making of activity plans as well as carrying them out and evaluating the results. In time planning, one's clock or watch helps measure time expenditure, while in energy planning knowledge of the energy costs of different activities, one's skill and ability to turn out work and the effects of fatigue help to measure energy expenditures. Though experience one learns how to work out well balanced, energy, spending patterns that are based on the store of energy available from day to day.

Controlling the Energy Plan:

Once the work plan in the use of energy is ready, the problem of how to implement it arises. The answer to this lies in the understanding and awareness of certain techniques related to body mechanics, work simplification, etc.

Motivation plays an important role in carrying out all activity plans, including those having to do with energy management. We have seen that high motivation makes more energy available for the tasks at hand, and helps control fatigue costs resulting from work.

Developing skills in fitting activities of daily living into the minutes and hours of the day conserves emotional and physical energy and stimulates greater efficiency in work. Skills of this kind lead to greater mental flexibility in the management of energy and in carrying out activity plans. Work simplification, the effective use of the body in housework and the skillful performance of homemaking tasks are the tools enable a homemaker to conserve time and energy so that more energy will be available for other interests and activities

Evaluating the Energy Used:

1. Asking oneself the following questions will help to evaluate success in utilizing one's store of energy:
2. Do I think of the use of energy in terms of the goals I wish to attain?
3. Do the energy costs of any homemaking tasks seem too high?
4. Am I using my energy effectively?
5. Have I worked out a well-balanced energy-spending pattern for both my homemaking and my other activities?
6. Do I often lengthen my work day in order to finish certain tasks?
7. What homemaking activities do I like best?
8. What do I dislike? Why do I dislike these activities?
9. How can I change my attitudes toward these activities?
10. What tasks are most tiring? Why?
11. Do I tire easily?
12. Do I recognize the type of fatigue I frequently experience?
13. Does it make me want to stop working?
14. What can I do to relieve fatigue?

15. Do I use effective methods of work to avoid fatigue?

16. Have I learnt to relax and rest?

17. An analysis of the answers to above questions would help a home-maker to evaluate whether she managing her energy resource properly or not.

5.10 Work Simplification

Introduction

At the turn of the 20th century when industry became interested in the efficiency of labor, the young wives of two efficient engineers brought the idea of improving work methods into the home under various names, the last of which was work simplification. The work can be simplified by applying the 'scientific management' process within and outside the home. Scientific management tells us how to analyze different jobs and identify where the inefficiency lies.

Anyone who is trying to lower time and energy expenditures soon learns the value of improving methods of work, because the time and energy required to do any task depend largely on the hand and body motions used. Improvement in the performance of a task usually means that the work is made easier because the new method is a more convenient one, permitting smooth, natural and rhythmical motions.

The term work simplification as used in the home is of a more for reaching nature than in industry and may even include omitting a task in its entirety. For example a bakery might apply work- simplification techniques to the method of making apple pies, but would not question making them as long as they have a profitable market. A home maker might similarly simplify her method of making an apple pie, but she might further simplify the task of preparing a dessert by making no apple pie but substituting baked apples. This latter in a fundamental sense is also work simplification.

The primary purpose of work simplification is to develop techniques that will reduce the allocation and minimize the use of your resources. The goal is to produce the highest degree of satisfaction with the least expenditure of resources while yielding the most desirable outcome.

The initial application of the principles of industrial work simplification to the household was done by Lillian Gilbreth who worked closely with her husband, Frank. Following his death, she and Christine Frederick continued this work. These two women were the forerunners of work simplification for the home.

In devising work simplification techniques one needs to become aware of the relationship of space, equipment, materials and supplies, physical structure and motion to the task being under taken. The knowledge of these relationships, one to another, assists in developing techniques to reduce or minimize resource consumption.

As long as the experienced homemaker is content with her daily activities and is able to complete her tasks without undue fatigue she has no reason to be concerned with work simplification. However, the woman who is bowed down with work either because she is gainfully employed or has heavy family responsibilities or the elderly woman and the incapacitated woman need work simplification.

Definition:

A given task is simplified by applying the scientific management techniques even at home. The Scientific management tells us how to analyse different jobs and identify what is inefficient. Nickell and Dorsey defined work simplification as "the conscious seeking of the simplest, easiest and quickest method of doing work". Gross and Crandall defined it as "accomplishing more work within a given amount of time and energy or at reducing the amount of either one or both to accomplish given amount of work". It implies proper blending and management of two important resources namely time and human energy.

Importance:

Work simplification presents a challenge to managers of all type of activities. Homemaking is an important and full time job for many homemakers. Many women who also hold jobs outside home face many demands on their time. Homemaking involves a special sort of labour known as house work, and it is essential to run the home.

The characteristics of household work show that:

(1) it is tedious, monotonous and time consuming;

(2) it needs lot of patience and various types of skills.

In view of these points it becomes more necessary to know how to simplify the work by acquiring knowledge of work simplification techniques applicable to different household tasks.

Work well done is satisfying and rewarding. But work inefficiently done, without skill and· under pressure, gives rise to frustration and unhappiness. A well managed home is necessary to happy family life. "Scientific management" means application of science to management problems. It includes the handling of machines, materials and people and it recognizes that of these three, people are the most important as they do the actual job. The use of scientific management is helpful. In order to conserve the human element, we must find out what is the one best way to do each job (Gilbreth, Thomas and Clymer, p. 4).

A homemaker has to perform many types of jobs to be one at home. She is often interrupted in her work, or she herself must interrupt in order to get to another job. In order to get everything done she may have to neglect her own social life or personal talents and hobbies for lack of time. She may suffer from physical fatigue, anxiety and tension due to heavy demands on her time and energy due to house chores.

The research studies have shown that by using work simplification one can reduce time given to one job; it can reduce the number of motions and improve type of motions on a specific task. It can reduce boredom of routine habits of work. It may fur!-her reduce frustration arising due to lack of effectiveness on a job.

Time and energy are closely related and if these are blended properly the work of the housewife will be much simplified. This can be achieved to a great extent by,

5.11   Techniques of Work Simplification

Work simplification and motion mindedness are the two important ways of reducing the time and energy expenditure and simplifying the work methods. Some of the scientific techniques used for motion and time studies are as follows:

1. Pathway chart
2. Process chart
3. Operation chart
4. Micro motion film analysis
5. Cyclegraph
6. Chronocyclegraph

1. The Pathway Chart:

It is a simple device for making the study of the path covered by the homemaker while doing a task. In this method a floor plan of the work area or room is drawn to scale and is fixed to a board on the wall. Some pins and string of thread are required to make such a study. At the starting point of the work one pin is inserted to the board. Thread is used to indicate the line of her motion and at each turning point of the homemaker a pin is put in the plan and the thread is wound around it.

After the completion of the task the length of the thread is measured. This will give an idea of the distances covered by the house wife. These are then studied to find out how they may be reduced. This technique helps to observe all unnecessary movements that can be reduced or eliminated. After a study of this process a revised plan with less movement can be made on another floor plan by which time and energy can be saved easily.

2. The Process Chart:

This is a step-by-step description of the method used in doing a task. Each task requires a specific process to be completed. In this technique a close study of the process is made. Ail unnecessary movements and steps made by the homemaker for doing n work are avoided by this technique.

3. The Operation Chart:

This is used to make a detailed study of a part of the activity of a work process. This technique helps one lo tract- out all unnecessary expenditure of time and energy in all activities. In this chart the movements of both hands, right and left are studied in great detail while doing one task. By the finer analysis, it can be easily known where unnecessary movements are being made and where the delays are occurring in the job. Both process charts and operation charts are useful motion and time study technique because they give very good results without using any special equipment.

4. Micro Motion Film Analysis:

In this technique motion picture of tasks done under normal condition are taken. Then it is analysed to study the finer movements of the hands and other parts of the body. A timing device may also be used to help for recording the time of the movement of the worker to complete the job.

5. The Cyclegraph:

It is a photographic device to the types of motions used in doing the task. When this is attached to some parts of the body, such as the hand during the time of ironing, it registers the pathway of light projected by a small electric bulb.

Analysis of the resulting photographic record of movements can show whether the movements are smooth and rhythmic or not. This is an effective way to learn how motions may be reduced and how methods of work may be improved while doing a task.

6. Chronocyclegraph:

In this method small lights are attached to the middle finger on each hand and the patterns of movement during a task are recorded on photographic film and analysed later. Motion and time studies have been made of each tasks as food preparation, dishwashing, laundering, ironing of clothes, bed making, cleaning and other tasks. These studies suggest many methods of simplifying homemakers in their own homes and analyzing where one can reduce the energy and time usage of the worker.

According to Mundel there are five levels of changes that can improve one's method of work:

1. Changes in body position, number and type of motions.
2. Changes in tools, working arrangements and equipment.
3. Changes in production sequence.
4. Changes in finished product.
5. Changes in the raw material.

Gross and Crandall combined these five classes of changes into three classes which are easily accepted by all.

These are:

1. Changes in Hand and Body Motions.
2. Changes in works and storage space and equipment.
3. Changes in the product.

1. Changes in Hand and Body Motions:

If attention will be given on the motions made by the hands and body, then time and energy can be saved easily.

This can be done by following methods:

(a) Eliminating unnecessary movements:

By adopting certain methods, unnecessary movements can be eliminated for e.g. Dishes are to be rinsed in a drainer and allowed them to dry without wiping. While preparing vegetables, they are to be put into the cooking vessels and thus handling of extra vessels is cut down. The towels, sheets and other linen should be arranged in order to save time and energy. Proper planning can save a number of movements between storage area and work space.

For e.g. when meals are being cooked the dining tables can be laid. Movements are also reduced when the floor is cleaned with a long handled mop, when clothes are placed at a convenient height at the time of drying. Keeping the house in smooth running order saves time and energy. Carrying several things at once to the kitchen or up and down stairs by the help of trays and baskets reduces unnecessary movements.

(b) Improving the sequence of work:

If the sequence of work will be improved, then movement required for a particular task can also be reduced. By following the pathway chart the sequence of works can be improved by reducing steps. Changes in the work methods can save unnecessary handling of equipment, e.g. when the dishes are stacked at the right of the sink washed, dried and stored at the left, minimum movements are required.

Various works in the kitchen can be grouped together. When dais are boiled, vegetables can be cut up or salads can be prepared. Cooking and Table Laying can be combined together. Ironing and mending can be done while foods are cooking. In cleaning the house, it is easier to finish each process of sweeping, dusting and mopping the floor in all the rooms than to clean each room separately.

(c) Developing skill in work:

The development of skill in the performance of homemaking tasks eliminates a number of time and energy consuming motions in a day's work. A skilled and experienced homemaker can do the tasks very easily with higher speed and smoothness. If the job is done with smooth rhythm, the efficiency of the home maker improves.

Each homemaker develops her own rhythm of doing work. Skill in work can be developed by learning, observation, effort and experience. For e.g. in learning to peel an apple, the home maker must first learn how to hold the apple and using the knife for peeling. This is a gradual improvement in developing the skill of doing the work through repetition. Making batter for pokoras, kneading dough and beating eggs are some examples of tasks involving rhythmic, uniform movements which can be learnt with experience.

(d) Comfortable Posture:

To avoid strain and to develop a good body position while working, some attention should be given to posture habits in standing, sitting; bending etc. working with good posture reduces the expenditure of energy. Poor posture can cause backache, increase fatigue, tension and a lower efficiency. Doing a task with efficient way means saving both time and energy e.g. in bending to do certain tasks, it is easier to put one foot slightly forward and bend through the knee and ankle joint. Carrying packages or other articles is easier when the load can rest against the hip.

2. Changes in Work and Storage Space and Equipment:

(a) Changes in equipment:

This includes rearranging or modifying kitchen equipment. For e.g. pressure cooker, mixer, grinder, well sharpened knives, peelers, rice cookers. Egg Beaters, non-stick pans, chapatti makers, dough mixers and other time and energy saving equipment help to ease the task of the homemaker. Now-a-days many modern, labour and time saving equipment's are available in the market which can be used easily.

(b) Changes in the work surface:

The height of kitchen work surfaces should be given careful attention. It must suit the worker. The platform on which the gas stove is placed should be in a suitable height. When the work surfaces in the kitchen are too low, one must stand in a comfortable position while working.

If the surfaces are too high, the arms and shoulders must be raised to make the adjustment to the height. When the work surfaces are too wide, it means stretching the arms and bending the body which cause unnecessary strain and fatigue. Grinding stones placed on the floor means additional bending and stretching.

According to Gilbreth, "The worker should stand erect with arms comfortably relaxed from the shoulders and with the elbows bent. She will find the most comfortable working level one, high enough to be used without stooping, but not high enough to cause her to raise the hands above the level of elbows.

Good Storage

(c) Changes in the storage space:

Storage areas in the kitchen and other places are often capable of being reorganized to help the homemaker to proceed better. Definite and convenient storage spaces enable the worker to do the kitchen work easily. Frequently used heavy utensils should be stored near the work surface level. All the tools, utensils, dishes and food supplies should be stored in such a way that they are readily accessible. Heavy articles should be placed at a lower height so that they are readily accessible.

3. Changes in the Product:

Work simplification through changes in the product depends upon the available resources and the family's standard of housekeeping. Most families have certain preconceived standard for housekeeping. Some ideas and habits of the families cannot be changed. But the homemaker should persuade the members to accept new ideas and change the old standard.

Some examples of these changes are as follows:

1. The use of paper napkins may help the busy urban working housewife who does not find time for laundering.

2. The purchase of prepared masala from a reliable source may save her from the older habit of picking, cleaning and grinding them at home daily.

3. Use of instant coffee will save her time and energy.

4. Clothes made of new fibers may be easier to maintain than traditional materials.

5. The use of plastics for some items may mean easily cleaned surfaces.

6. Laminated table tops are kept clean easily are heat resistant and easily maintained.

7. Instead of preparing an elaborate fruit salad as a dessert for a meal, whole fruits may be served.

8. A housewife, who is in the habit of ironing all the garments including the undergarments at home, can iron only the outer garments.

A part from all these steps, a genuine liking for the job, developing competent skills for the job, and the determination to carry it through, will be great assets in work simplification planning work with adequate rest periods would ensure better quality of work and less fatigue.

List of References

1. Betty B. Swanson 1981, <u>Introduction</u> to Home Management, Macmillan publishing co., Inc. New York.
2. Deacon, R, & Firebaugh, F.(1988), Family Resource management: Principles and Applications (2nd edition) , Boston: Allyn &bacon
3. DR. V.V.Bharathi and Ms. M, <u>Family</u> Resource <u>Management</u> (New Concepts and Theory) Discovery Publishing House New Delhi.
4. Gross And Crandall And Knoll.,Management for Modern families. Third edition. Prentice Hall, Inc, Englewood Cliffs, New Jersey pp:392.
5. Irma H. Gross , Elizabeth Walbert Crandall and Marjorie M. Knoll, 1973, Management for Modern Families (third edition) Prentice- Hall, Inc., Englewood Cliffs, New Jersey
6. Key, R.,& Firebough, F.(1989), Family resource management: Preparing for the 21st century, journal of home economics,81(p),13-17
7. Nickell.P, Rice, A.S. and Tucker, S.P. 1942. Management in family living(5th ed), New York, John Wiley And Sens.
8. Nickell, Paulena and Dorsey Jean M, 1970, Management in Family Living, New Delhi. Wiley Eastern Ltd.
9. P.CTripathi and P.N Reddy 1983, Principles of Management (Third Edition), Tata McGraw-Hill Publishing Company Limited, New Delhi
10. Premavathy Seetharaman, Sonia Batra and Preeti Mehra 2005, An Introduction to Family Resource Management, CBS Publishers and Distributors, New Delhi
11. Premavathy Seetharaman, And Mohini Sethi 2002, Consumerism Strategies and Tactics, CBS Publishers and Distributors, New Delhi.
12. Rose E.Steidl And Esther Crew Bratton 1968, Work in the Home, John Wiley and sons, New York
13. Rose E.Steidl And Esther Crew Bratton 1968, Work in the Home, John Wiley and sons, New York
14. Ruth E Deacon and Francille M. Firebaugh 1975, Home Management Context and Concepts, Houghton Mifflin Company, New Jersey
15. Varghese, M. A., Ogale n. N. and Srinivasan K. 1985, Home <u>Management</u>, New Age International (P) Limited, Publishers New Delhi
16. http://www.yourarticlelibrary.com/home-management/home-science-work-simplification-methods-with-diagram/47806/
17. http://www.nios.ac.in/media/documents/sechmscicour/english/home%20science%20(eng)%20ch-15.pdf
18. http://www.familyresourcemanagement.org/services/characteristics-of-resources/

19. http://www.familyresourcemanagement.org/services/management/
20. http://www.textbooksonline.tn.nic.in/books/12/std12-homesci-em.pdf
21. http://ecoursesonline.iasri.res.in/mod/page/view.php?id=122332